Just a Process

# Just a Process

## Views on the Relations between Research, Practice and Politics in the Sector of VET

### Festschrift for Anja Heikkinen

Edited by Philipp Gonon,
Lorenz Lassnigg
and Manfred Wahle

PETER LANG
EDITION

**Bibliographic Information published by the Deutsche Nationalbibliothek**
The Deutsche Nationalbibliothek lists this publication in the Deutsche Nationalbibliografie; detailed bibliographic data is available in the internet at http://dnb.d-nb.de.

Photo: University of Tampere, Winter 2012
© Manfred Wahle

ISBN 978-3-631-64438-6 (Print)
E-ISBN 978-3-653-03062-4 (E-Book)
DOI 10.3726/978-3-653-03062-4


Peter Lang Edition is an Imprint of Peter Lang GmbH.

Peter Lang – Frankfurt am Main · Bern · Bruxelles · New York · Oxford · Warszawa · Wien



www.peterlang.com

# Exposition

This book is dedicated to Anja Heikkinen by some of her international friends and colleagues. The call to contribute was issued in November 2011, with the ambitious goal to be published in February 2012. Indeed, a preliminary version was presented to her at a seminar in Tampere around her Birthday with the title "*The personal and the political*".

Once asked about her expectation concerning an anniversary publication celebrating her 60th birthday, Anja answered: "My colleagues and friends shall write what they have always wanted to tell me." The idea was to focus on the VET & Culture Network (http://peda.net/veraja/uta/vetculture), one of Anja's "life-projects" that celebrated its 20th anniversary in Tampere in June 2013. It was not so much meant to be a traditional scientific publication and it should include essays on the contributors' personal relationship with Anja in academic life respectively in the context of the VET & Culture Network. The book should focus on the following topics:

- Reflecting and remembering common activities with Anja in the context of the network
- Stories of network members as a personal perspective on the network's identity
- Relations between research, practice, and politics.

We think that the volume has achieved its goals by giving a lively account of the development and the activities of the network, and also of some of the topics its members have always been struggling with. Somehow the personal chapters also provide views about the informal processes behind the forming and evolvement of such a network of researchers, which has only relied on the personal interests and engagement of its members.

The first five chapters give personal impressions about the development of the network from different starting points and under different perspectives: How to become an expert in a new professional field (*C.Düsseldorff*)? What does travelling mean in today's Europe (*B.Niemeyer*)? Personal and sociological explorations of the meanings of time and space for education, research, and networking (*R.Husemann & M.Vesala-Husemann*), including some memories about the times when Anja had to defend her doctoral thesis – and greetings from Lapland (*A.Lindgren*). A history of the evolving topics and questions in the work of the network, related to the increasing inflow of contributing colleagues, are discussed by *L.Mjelde & M.Wahle*. *M.Weil* gives a reflection on his experience in an international cross-cultural higher education teaching experiment supported by ERASMUS (http://www.peda.net/veraja/jyu/kastdk/emvet/crosslife). The six contributions in the second part discuss some topics, which have always been important in the network, and try to take up open questions and find new ways of answering them: dealing with politics and institutions (*L.Lassnigg, K.Kraus, O.J.Olsen*), gender and vocationalism (*L.Mjelde, M.Wahle*), history and comparisons (*M.Vonken*), and transitions (*P.Gonon*). Very much can be read between the lines about how this community of research in VET has evolved during the decades, and how it struggles to proceed.

With the publication of the contributions to the workshops and conferences, predominantly in the Peter Lang Series '*Studies in Vocational and Continuing Education*' edited by Anja Heikkinen together with Philipp Gonon, some lasting contributions to the field have been made. We also must say that the VET & Culture Network has been a big endeavour of Anja, however, it does only account for one part of her work. Several other important contributions, among them her work on adult education in her home country Finland, or her engagement in teaching and professional-political matters in her academic homes, are not documented in this volume.

Many thanks for all your stimulating and challenging contributions and interventions, and good luck!

Philipp Gonon, Lorenz Lassnigg, and Manfred Wahle,
Zurich, Vienna, and Wuppertal, July 2013

# Table of Contents

# Before the Network was born: Expert meets Non-Experts

*Christina Düsseldorff*

In the late summer of 1990, the Berlin Wall was just knocked down; we (2 women, 2 men and a dog) lived in flat-sharing community in Bochum. One of them was my brother. After a long period as squatters everybody was lucky to live a peaceful life in our new and comfortable flat. At that time my brother worked as a doctor student at the chair of Karlwilhelm Stratmann at the Ruhr University in Bochum. Stratmann, one of the VET & Culture Network founders, once asked him, if we could shelter a young lady from Finland for a few months. She would like to come to Germany to do some research in VET for preparing her doctor thesis. As we were told, she did not have much money, something we were familiar with. Our community was used to host people in our flat. It was an open house where mainly artists, dancers or puppet-players with little money found a place to stay during their guest performance. But also other people came to stay for whatever reason.

At that time I just had started to work in GDR (which still existed until October 1990). As my new job was 700 km apart from Bochum near the border to Poland I only came back home for the week end. So we decided to offer the empty room to the young researcher. The only thing we knew about our future cohabitant from Finland was her name: Anja.

At the time Anja arrived I was already working in the east of Germany. I cannot tell anything about the beginning of her stay in Bochum. But I remember very well when I met her the first time. I arrived at home on an early Friday evening before dinner time. The common dinner had an important value in our living together. We were all ambitious cooks with joy to experiment and not each of us was always successful. But whatever was served, table cloth, china, candle and a bottle of red wine never was missing when we all came together, and we had mostly a long session. In this respect we were very bourgeois.

Of course I was very curious to meet our new occupant. When I entered the kitchen one whispered to me: “Tonight it is your turn!” I didn’t understand a word. What does it mean: “your turn?” I already had noticed that everybody looked a little bleary-eyed, so I asked: “Is there anything wrong with Anja?” “She keeps on asking questions about the Germany education system and never wants to go to bed!” - Going to bed very late never had been a problem before in our house. I became a little uncertain. Then we had dinner. We talked about this and that and finishing the last course one after the other said good night. I stayed with Anja sharing a bottle of red wine and answering questions about the education system in East and West Germany till the early morning. This was the night when I got to know Anja.

Anja stayed in our house for a couple of months. Discussions about education became part of our life. Meanwhile not only my brother was an expert in education, because this was his job; but also the others: Sabine und Klaus as puppet-players and me, the jurist. Only the dog seemed to be untouched from this subject. Many bottles of wine were emptied before Anja left. She came back another time to stay with us for a couple of weeks. Maybe she had enjoyed her first visit.

## Ten years later: How to become a researcher in VET?

Time went by, the community became history and from time to time I heard something about Anja on her professional development without having any personal contact. May be the saying is true: "You always meet twice". In this case it became evident. In 2002 I started to work at the Institute for Commercial Education/Vocational Education & Training/University of Duisburg as a project manager. It was my task to manage a huge EU funded research project for three years and the fact that the new job was located in the section of pedagogy was more or less a coincidence. After a period of learning, how university administration works (or does not work), new challenges became necessary, because this administrative work was not fulfilling. In addition to my management-job I soon was integrated into a team for evaluating the current curricula of vocational education in the transportation sector and as well in the program evaluation of "Learning Regions". Here I came in touch with the theory of networking.

With these new tasks I had to become a researcher in vocational education and training. Besides reading books and articles to cover the actual job demands, I decided to meet other researchers to listen to them, to learn as much as possible and to understand their attitude as researcher etc. Of course in my age career plans to become a researcher in a subject I was not familiar with could not be very ambitious, and for a longer time I was not convinced to go on with my job at the university. But the change from an outsider to an insider became more and more important. Therefore being included into the network seemed to be crucial for me in this situation. So the idea was born to join the VET & Culture Network, where international experts could be found. Of course I was a little afraid to go to the first meeting in Mustiala as a non-expert, but the fact that I knew Anja and some other net workers made the decision easier to go there.

My ambitious plan to become an expert in education can be assessed as "partly successful". In my review as a participant of eight network meetings I would say: I learned a lot in the VET & Culture Network and also many things I didn't expect before.

## Mustiala 2003 (Educating the ostriches)

The first thing I learned here was: It is not easy to get to the remote places, where the VET & Culture net workers use to meet. Good knowledge in geography and creativity in travel organizing are key competences for a successful arrival. Even the Finnish taxi driver lost his orientation on his way through the wood to the vocational training school for farming near Mustiala, where the meeting took place. When Anja organizes a meeting (and this is also true for some other organizers, as I found out later), she uses to choose places in the nature far away from traditional conference luxury. I remember well when we picked up two German colleagues from the next bus station to help them finding the vocational training school. We got stuck in the wood with their wheeled suitcases. The colleague's high heeled shoes and her dark blue suit were also not suitable for this cross-walk. A warm jumper and walking shoes instead are a must for network meetings because sitting outside at a fireplace is a necessary part of the program.

The second thing I learned here was something about behaviorism: When I tried to make friends with the ostriches, who lived in the farming area of the training school, I offered them a dandelion leaf. After a few visits the brave ones took the leaf and even came to the fence when they saw me coming. The other birds stood nearby and watched the scene. When we became familiar I changed the setting and offered five leafs at once. The ostriches became nervous, twinkled with their eyes and were unable to select one leaf out of the bundle. I reduced the number of leafs and found out that only the clever one could select among two leafs. The birds were hopelessly overtaxed with a greater selection. One thing I could not explain to myself: How can these animals survive in the nature, because the ground, where they pick their food, is full of leaves with even a greater variety? May be not every theory can give a sufficient answer to important questions in real life.

## Oslo 2004 (Shellfish on the boat party)

The first thing I learned here was something about intercultural differences: The reaction of rainy weather depends of the cultural background and the interpretation of this reaction or behavior is afflicted with prejudices. When we arrived at the conference place, a house from the Norwegian trade union in the middle of woods, it was cold and raining cats and dogs. When we finished unloading the car the rain stopped a little and we decided to explore the area where the conference took place. On our way we saw a tall middle aged man coming out of the wood, rising up his arms and screaming: "How nice and green, how nice and green!" Our first idea was: Poor man, he might have a mental problem. He came towards us, shacked hands and said: "My name is Peter from Australia".

The second thing I learned here was: The proper eating of shellfish might show once refinement. To eat shellfish with cold fingers on a rolling boat in a Norwegian Fjord may show the eater's lack of culture but it is a pleasure.

## Joensuu 2005 (Watching the northern lights)

The first thing I learned was: VET and Culture net workers are not only capable in theory of co-operation and the organization of work. They also can put it into practice. Grilling sausages on an open camp fire are well liked events in the social program for net workers. Of course the preparation needs teamwork. Not only the cooperative wood collecting but also the cooking process itself (beside the drinks) is very important for a positive group experience. But when 20 hungry people try to hold their sausages into a small camp fire there is a danger of interfering each other and this might end up into a mess when the sausage falls from the stick into the fire. The transfer of knowledge about the organization of lean production lines can help VET researchers to make the collective sausage grill successful. So the transfer of theory into practice is essential for real life.

The second thing I learned here was: The lifelike description of an impressive natural phenomenon by mobile phone after having a couple of drinks can produce irritation to the recipient who is not watching the scene. So before you want to share an event with somebody else over a long distance you should take into account that the other person may have its own interpretation of this description due to his specific horizon. Peter's telephone call to his wife in Australia about the description of the northern lights with the changing colours of the sky from yellow to green and then to violet was a good example that sender and recipient need the same context for a common understanding because the perception of changing colours in the sky may have different reasons.

## Konstanz 2007 (The transnational network meeting)

The first thing I learned here was: A network meeting with participants from all over the world can be transnational in a double meaning when the locations of the meeting are cross border. I doubt that the non European participants were always aware, which national VET system was in discussion but it showed at least the options we could have in an open Europe if we use them in a better way.

The second thing I learned here was: Even if VET researchers are sitting in the same boat (on the Lake Constance) it does not mean that we share the same problems. In comparison with the colleagues in Africa our work conditions are much better.

## Arvidsjaur 2008 (Risky learning methods)

The first thing I learned here was: Using common vocational training methods can be sometimes risky and demands courage from teacher and learner. Learning by doing is essential for a successful training, but to learn how to act in a critical situation. Engine stop during a flight is usually trained on a flight simulator to reduce the risk. In Lapland the flying instructor stops the engine during the flight and watches the trainee pilot's reaction.

The second thing I learned here was: Problems of VET can be discussed anywhere and you find partners for discussion in places you never expected before. On our excursion through the woods in Lapland near the Arctic Circle we met some people sitting round a fireplace for a picnic. They offered us a coffee which was prepared on the open fire and started with a discussion about education. It came out that they have read about the VET & Culture Network meeting in the local newspaper and as pedagogues themselves they did not want to miss the chance for an exchange of views about actual problems in VET in an international perspective.

## Zürich 2009 (Salad, or the 'worst case')

The first thing I learned here was: The vocational school, where the meeting took place, was very well equipped and seemed to show the value of vocational education in Switzerland. I would like to know if this is true everywhere in the country or if we only saw a "lighthouse" in a rich region.

The second thing I learned here was: Reading a word in a foreign language and pronouncing it in the mother tongue may create a new word, which is appropriate to the situation coincidently. As Switzerland is an extremely expensive place to live, we decided to go to a small snack bar for dinner to save our travel budget. For an Australian the menu in German language was difficult to understand, so he tried to select his order according to the price. "I take the *Worst Case Salad*". The offer in the menu was *"Wurst-Käse-Salat"*, a typical cold dish in Switzerland, which is made from sausages *(Wurst)* and cheese *(Käse)*. It has nothing to do with a worst case but it may describe the situation.

## Hattingen 2010 (The Intellectual Agenda)

The first thing I learned here was: Being responsible for the planning and carrying out a VET & Culture Network meeting is not easy. The preparation takes time, needs creativity, and the response of the networker, who is going to participate, comes only slowly. But when everybody has arrived the networkers are really team players and in most cases easy to handle.

The second thing I learned here was: In a globalized world virtual money can be transferred within a few seconds with a simple click on the computer from one end of the world to the other. But the hurdles for changing some real existing Hong Kong Dollars into real existing EUROs in the heart of Europe are very high. You need a bank account in the local bank. There is still enough potential for innovation in the bank sector.

## Torino 2011(ETF)

The first thing I learned here was: In an institution with international staff there is not automatically intercultural competence to fulfill the tasks. It is a question of awareness that the transfer of knowledge in the education sector (and elsewhere) cannot be a one way road. Without a partnership with local partners at eye level the transfer cannot be successful because the local or national peculiarity is left out of consideration. May be this is something which is not always on the agenda of EU policy.

The second thing I learned here was: VET & Culture networkers are very flexible and adaptable. They cannot only find their way to remote places for network meetings. They also make a good impression in a cosmopolitan city. Even there they find a way for their specific way of networking.

## Conclusion

Reflecting all the network meetings over the years I have to consider that I learned much more than the things mentioned above. Anja and the network always played a central role in this learning process. I feel far away to be an expert in VET because I still have a lack of knowledge in many fields of this subject. But on the other hand I reflect on questions and themes in a way I would not have done in my daily work without the impetus of the network. So the network has opened my professional horizon and I met friends. It might have been the friendly atmosphere in the discourse which lets me feel as an insider now. This is something Anja could not have foreseen when we were sitting more than twenty years ago at our table with our bottle of red wine and I was examined about the German education system.

# Never despise humble beginnings

*Liv Mjelde and Manfred Wahle*

## 1. On the beginnings of the VET & Culture Network (Liv Mjelde)

Years ago, I received an invitation from Anja Heikkinen. This was in late October, 1993. She asked me if I would attend a workshop on Vocational Education at the University of Tampere from the 16 to the 20 of November 1993. I had defended my doctoral dissertation called "Apprenticeship. From Practice to Theory and Back Again" on October 8th of that year at the University of Joensuu in Eastern Finland. I remember that the University of Joensuu did not have money to pay their employees that year. The Finnish state was deeply mired in debt and their loans from Germany were sky high. In the middle of this crisis, someone by the name of Anja Heikkinen had miraculously managed to find money to invite scholars to discuss the problems of vocational and technical education. The venue was Hämeenlinna.

There were not many of us who gathered in Tampere during those dark November days. We were a handful of scholars from Germany, England, Finland and Norway. I remember very well the small classroom where we met. "But never despise humble beginnings" said one of the Nobel Prize Winners, Leymah Gbowee from Liberia in 2011. She had mobilized and organized women to end the civil war being conducted by power-hungry men in Liberia. The women had started with 10 dollars in cash and they made miracles, literally out of nothing. The war ended and Charles Taylor had to give in. They then worked to secure women's participation in parliamentary and presidential elections. As a result largely of their labours, Liberia was the first country in the history of Africa to elect a woman president, Ellen Johnsen Sirleaf in 2006. Those two women were awarded the Nobel Peace Prize in 2011 together with Tawakkul Karman from Yemen.

### Who was there?

Back to Finland and our humble beginnings. It was Karlwilhelm Stratmann and Manfred Wahle who came from the University of Bochum, Germany. Karlwilhelm Stratmann was the grand old man in the field of the history of vocational education in Germany, especially on the dual system. He and Manfred Wahle were also running an important research project on vocational education and youth policy in "Kaiser Wilhelm's Reich". How did the system intend to train the growing working class, both in schools and in work places in the old Kaiser-Reich? Richard Aldrich and Andy Green represented England. Richard Aldrich was the chairperson of the Department of Philosophy, History and Humanities in the Institute of Education, University of London. He is a well-known scholar and has published widely on the history of British education. Andy Green was posted in the Post-16 Education Centre also at the University of London. He was a specialist on comparative research in vocational education, especially between UK, France, Japan and USA.

Finland had of course the biggest contingent. Ari Antikainen was Professor of Sociology of Education at the University of Joensuu. He headed two historical/ sociological projects; "Searching for the Meaning of Education in Finnish Society" and "Towards a Learning Society". They were huge longitudinal, empirical research projects. On these projects he was assisted by others who attended: Jarmo Houtsonen, Hannu Huotelin and Juha Kauppila. Then there was Jorma Enkenberg, a physicist, an assistant professor in the Department of Subject/Teacher Training at the University of Joensuu. He was working on developing simulative learning strategies in the training of computer science teachers. Mervi Kaarninen was a researcher in the Department of History at the University of Tampere. Her work was on the history of the education of Finnish girls in the 1920s and 1930s. Juha Nieminen was connected to the Department of Education at the University of Tampere and he worked on the history of Finnish youth work. Anja Heikkinen was at that time a lecturer of vocational education and she worked on the cultural aspects of vocational education, exemplified by the formation of the development of Finnish vocational education in crafts and industry in the period between 1840/1940. I am a sociologist, and I brought with me my speciality, the sociology of education, particularly Norwegian vocational education and apprenticeship learning.

What strikes me when I consider the background of the participants in this first VET conference is the variation in our backgrounds. We were educationalists but mainly educated as historians and sociologists, and also a physicist working on teacher education. The question of what kind of influence history should have on sociology and vice versa is an interesting topic in general. There seems to have been a variation of outlooks on these questions in the hegemonic world, both in time and space over the course of the past century. Social scientists such as Jürgen Habermas, Ralf Dahrendorf and Rainer Lepsius had historical interests a generation ago. It looks like the social scientists of today tend to orient themselves less towards historical perspectives. The way I see it, you cannot grasp the development of vocational education and culture without both historical and sociological perspectives. It seems that Finnish social scientists have grasped these perspectives in an exemplary way. I am thinking of the works of Ari Antikainen and Leena Koski at the University of Joensuu, as well as that of Anja Heikkinen who had these perspectives when she initiated the network with that invitation to Hämeenlinna in 1993. She saw the need for an historical and comparative understanding of the development of vocational education in Europe. She saw that vocational education was generally a neglected research field in European educational science. She saw the need for doing comparative research and the need for having an understanding of the cultural and historical context in different countries. She saw the need for training young researchers to do research in vocational education and the need for a joint endeavor. She also said that such efforts must not, however, neglect the wider global perspective on vocational education. On the contrary, it should make us move away from monistic, nationally restricted studies, and move toward comparisons, towards a reflective dialogue on the similarity and differences in the cultural characteristics of vocational education in different countries. She also stressed that a dialogue between different academic traditions is a prerequisite for an understanding of the peculiarities of European vocational education in a wider context.

## The topics

The presentations at that first meeting created lively, inspiring and broad-based discussions.[1] Karlwilhelm Stratmann dealt with the change of what constituted the dominating ideas in the formation of skills for the manual labour market over a long historical period in Germany. He showed how the ideas that dominated and guided apprenticeship education in feudal times changed in the transition towards industrial production during a lengthy span of economic and political liberalism. The family-like feudal socialization into craftsmanship changed gradually into industrial, sequenced, individual qualifications employed to form a skilled industrial worker. Manfred Wahle showed how local social groups, such as Protestant societies for youth protection, the welfare-organization of factory owners and merchant organizations were most important in "Youth Salvation Campaigns" in the Kaiserian Reich (1871-198). Richard Aldrich discussed "the failure of vocational education and training" in Britain. He showed in general how the occupational and educational ideas of the elite had determined the

1 See Heikkinen Anja (edt) 1994. Vocational Education and Culture.European Prospects from History and Life History. Hämeenlinna: Tampereen Yliopiston Hämeenlinnan Opettajankoulutuslaitos

development of schooling in Britain. He also pointed out the paradigmatic change that had occurred in educational policy and thinking during the Thatcher era. Andy Green discussed on his work in the field of "Technical Education and State Formation in Nineteenth Century England and France," stressing how the French state system established a national system of technical education in France while England, with its pioneering role in the industrial revolution, never created any coherent system. Ari Antikainen and Jarmo Houtsonen discussed the possibilities of finding personal meaning of education from oral histories. Hannu Huotelin and Juha Kauppila presented the meaning of education to four different generations. Mervi Kaarninen looked into the vocational educational and occupational life course of a group of working class girls in Tampere during the inter-war period. She shows how domestic ideology of the 1920s and 1930s was the most important factor affecting girls' educational structures as well as the curriculum. Juha Nieminen presented three traditions of organized Youth Work in Finland and their conceptualizations of youth. Anja Heikkinen gave an interpretation of why schooling had become a set of characteristic organizing and educational principles in vocational education in Finland.

Jorma Enkenberg in his work "Situated Cognition and Cognitive Apprenticeship" discussed reasons of why so little attention has been paid to the processes the masters/experts are engaged in when they carry out complex tasks and how to develop a pedagogical practice where teachers and students develop their cognitive skills in order to develop problem solving learning situations. He asked about the interaction between theoretical knowledge and practical knowledge in learning of high level practical skills and how to conceptualize learning in general - especially when wanting to develop powerful computer programs for learners. He discussed the scientific shift towards an understanding of cognitivism towards situated cognition and how learning is looked upon as a process of interpretation and situated in people's experience in their everyday lives. I discussed the relationship between intellectual and manual labour, between work of hand and work of mind and between vocational learning and academic learning traditions as the underlying concern in the school reforms in Norway after the Second World War, seen in the light of my empirical research among apprentices in Norway and their experience of learning in schools and learning in work places. I discussed this against the work of Lev Vygotsky and his historical and dialectical analysis toward an understanding of human development and mental activity. Vygotsky's interpretations have huge consequences for ways of understanding the phylogenic and ontogenic development of human beings. I have used this understanding in my analysis of the contradictions in the development in the educational system in the transition from feudal to industrial ways of organizing labour and learning and how vocational students and apprentices experience their everyday learning life in schools and workplaces.

How human beings learn is of course the central problem in psychology; Science has come far in the past decades towards a deeper understanding of human beings' cognitive functions. My experiences with Finland, its culture, activities and history have enriched my understanding of vocational pedagogy in general. For instance, I am aware that Finland is well known for their development of systematic thinking in the field of activity theory, following up the scientific work of Lev Vygotsky and A.R. Luria. The development of the material conditions that laid the groundwork for perceptual differences in class society and different ways of learning are central in the Soviet researcher A.R. Luria's work.

Fiction may however often be more "scientific than science" in their description of societal development. In Norway we have the Danish/Norwegian writer Aksel Sandemose who has sociological dimensions in his writing. He was born in Denmark, but lived in Norway most of his life. But one of the greatest in the Nordic countries in this respect might be the Finnish writer Vainø Linna. He has in his trilogy "Under the North Star" taken up the historical-philosophical and social problems in the development of Finnish modern history. It encompasses every important event in the country's history from the 1890s to the 1950s from the point of view of people's everyday life, the difference between rich and poor and the struggles for decent ways of life. As readers of Linna's work, we follow the destiny of a crofter family and the emergence of family members as independent farmers. The trilogy gives the dramatic history of Finland from the 1880's until after World War 2. The writer paints a vast fresco of the destiny of Finland from the pressure of Czarist Russia through the war of independence, the Civil War, the depression of the 1930's, the oppression and bewilderment of the Winter War and World War 2. It is said that this novel gave the Finns a more true understanding of their own history than what had been presented to them from the academic world. It reminds me of Bernardo Bertolucci's epic film "1900." That film covers seventy years of Italian social and political history, from 1901, when the peasants were still in bondage to the landowners, and proceeds to the end of World War 2. The film is a realistic, three-generational portrayal of the relationship between landowners and crofters in the Italian country side. These two works portray similar struggles on the northern and southern edges of Europe.

Thanks to the VET conferences, we were given the opportunity to visit the place Vainø Linna was born in 1920, in Urjala in south-western Finland and this area (his very own 'back yard' was used as the setting for his epic work). On both sides of his family he descended from western Finnish crofter and farm labourers. He moved at the age of 17 to Tampere, Finland's largest industrial town, where he got a job in a textile factory. Tampere, now that industrial production has moved elsewhere, houses the University of Tampere. It is a city marked by big struggles during the civil war. It also has a Lenin Museum. Lenin and Stalin met for the first time in Tampere in preparation for the road to proletarian power in Russia. The VET delegation visited the museum in 1995. Finland then talked about closing the museum. A Finnish television team was present and they interviewed me about the proposed closing of the museum. I advised against the closure. It is an important part of Finnish history as well as world history. Finland also got its independence from Czarist Russia as a result of the Russian Revolution.

Back to VET & Culture, the next conference took place, again in Hämeenlinna, in June 1995.[2] I remember we lived in a hotel that was run by a vocational school. The students had their praxis in the hotel, as receptionists, chamber maids, cooks and waiters. The aim of the workshop was to integrate discussions with practitioners. Some new researchers had joined us, Philipp Gonon from Switzerland, Rudolf Husemann from Germany and Ronald Sultana from Malta, as well as Michael Young, Alan Venters and David Crook from England. There were also new people from Finland, Leena Kuusisto, Riitta Narko, Maija Vesala and Paivi Venalainen.

The first conference we had outside Finland was in Malta in September 1996. Ronald Sultana had been working on education and national development with historical and critical perspectives on vocational education in Malta and we had been in contact for years. The University of Malta invited the VET group to their elegant guest house in 1997. We were there from Finland, Germany, Malta, Norway and Switzerland. Apprenticeship in Europe was at the core of the discussions. The old concept with its varying connotations and prestige had experienced a remarkable rehabilitation, symbolizing emerging new ways of understanding vocational education and training and the relation between education and work in Europe.[3]

2 See Heikkinen, Anja 1995: Vocational Education and Culture. European Prospects from Theory and Practice. Hämeenlinna: Tampereen Yliopiston Hämeenlinnan Opettajankoulutuslaitos

3 See Heikkinen, Anja & Ronald Sultana (eds) Vocational Education and Practices in Europe. Challenges for Practice and Research. Tampere: University of Tampere.

## 2. On further details of humble beginnings (Manfred Wahle)

As Liv Mjelde points out in the chapter above, the history of the VET & Culture Network and its further developments started at the workshop in Hämeenlinna in 1993. To complete the story of humble beginnings, this chapter deals with further details of the origin of the VET & Culture Network.

In this respect, an important date is the year 1991. Looking back to the history of the network, it is also necessary to recall Karlwilhelm Stratmann (1930-1997) briefly. Stratmann was a professor of vocational education and the chair of vocational pedagogies *(Berufs- und Wirtschaftspädagogik)* at the University of Bochum. He published numerous articles and books on the German system of vocational education and training, especially on its history, ideological and pedagogical legitimating and formation. Stratmann was one of the most important mentors of historical research on vocational education and training in Germany, and he had an immense influence on this discipline. Furthermore, he made a principle of supporting young researchers and also of giving them access to academic life. Thus, I worked as one of the responsible researchers in a research-project on vocational education and youth policy in Kaiserian Germany (*Deutsches Kaiserreich*, 1870-1918). This project lasted from 1991 till 1995. The person in charge of the project was Karlwilhelm Stratmann. My participation in the project was the continuation of working at his chair since 1980, when I had signed my first contract of employment with Stratmann.

At the same time when I was running the project on the history of the working class youth in Germany, Anja Heikkinen was finishing her doctoral thesis on cultural aspects of vocational education and training, exemplified by the formation of Finnish vocational education and training in crafts and industry during 1840-1940. Regarding this, her research did not just focus on Finnish matters but also on outer influences during the formation of the Finnish system of vocational education and training. Thus, she also made research on classic pedagogical and sociological theories and historical German concepts on (vocational) education. In this context, Anja Heikkinen got connected with Karlwilhelm Stratmann as an outstanding expert of classic theories in vocational education and training of the times: e.g. those of Friedrich Daniel Ernst Schleiermacher (1768-1834), Johann Heinrich Pestalozzi (1746-1827), Georg Kerschensteiner (1854-1932) and Eduard Spranger (1882-1963). Finally Anja Heikkinen was invited by Karlwilhelm Stratmann in 1991 to continue her research on the history of vocational education and to discuss any issues of this object. Thus, one day she arrived in Bochum.[4]

With that the story about my connection with Anja Heikkinen began. In connection with this, the following is interesting to know. At the chair of vocational pedagogies at the University of Bochum all members of Karlwilhelm Stratmann's research team, that means each assistant lecturer and lecturer, each of his master- and doctoral students and even his secretary were obliged to participate in his *Oberseminar*, which has already become almost legendary. This was an advanced seminar on a high academic level with the demand to extend the knowledge about theories, concepts and both pedagogical and political challenges in the field of vocational education and training. The seminar was held each Thursday from 6.00 until 8.00 o'clock p.m. Of course, it had to happen that Anja Heikkinen was obliged to participate in Stratmann's *Oberseminar*, too.

However, connected to the *Oberseminar* another tradition was established. Subsequent to the seminar most of the researchers carried on the discussion in a pub. Additional to many other discussions during Anja Heikkinen's first stay in Bochum in 1991 and her second stay at the University of Bochum in 1993, I had several meetings with her. Although not only these discussions were deciding to promote the idea of continuing transnational cooperation in VET research, a result of them was that this idea had gradually won a distinct profile. Putting this concept into practice, Anja Heikkinen invited handful of scholars to a workshop on vocational education at the University of Tampere in the middle of November 1993. At this workshop I had a presentation about some results of my research in the project mentioned above.[5] Finally, this workshop, which was organized and coordinated by Anja Heikkinen, was the birthday of the VET & Culture Network. It was also the starting point to develop both continuing and widening transnational cooperation in VET research.

4 With regard to Anja's stay in Bochum in 1991 in greater detail see Christina Düsseldorff's essay in this book.

5 See Heikkinen Anja (ed) 1994. Vocational Education and Culture. European Prospects from History and Life History. Hämeenlinna: Tampereen Yliopiston Hämeenlinnan Opettajankoulutuslaitos, 153-176

*First row: Liv Mjelde, Anja Heikkinen (left to right)*
*Second row: Manfred Wahle, Jarmo Houtsonen, Karlwilhelm Stratmann (left to right)*

*During the first workshop on Vocational Education at the University of Tampere (Nov. 1993)*

*First row left to right : Karlwilhelm Stratmann, Anja Heikkinen, Jarmo Houtsonen, Ari Antikainen,*
*Second row left to right: Manfred Wahle, Liv Mjelde, Hannu Huotelin, Juha Kauppila*

## 3. Review on the activities of the VET & Culture Network from 1993 to the present (Manfred Wahle)

Since 1993 the VET & Culture Network has won its unique profile. If the first initiatives of creating the network had represented humble beginnings beyond usual pathways, nevertheless they had been very significant for future activities, as strengthening the international cooperation towards a structural optimum or expanding common projects. Concerning this, during the first workshops respectively conferences in 1993 and 1995 a core group of networkers had grown together. Since then this group has been responsible for the further development of the network, and especially Anja Heikkinen has played a main role in the whole project from the beginnings till this day.

Simultaneously the number of researchers who stick to the VET & Culture Network has increased continuously. Besides other facts, this is reflected by the particularity that the thematic structure of the network facilitates the integration of discussions with practitioners into each annual conference and workshop. By that a tradition of the network has been carried on up to the present: conferences and workshops bring experiences and perspectives from educational practice as contributions from administration, politics, and educators into the discussion of (comparative) studies on various forms of vocational education and training from various disciplinary areas of educational science like history, sociology and philosophy of education.

Nevertheless, over the years the character of the network has changed. If not its concept and demand but at least its outward appearance has differed visibly from the beginnings to date. The more the network had lost its initial property as a predominantly informal cooperation of VET researchers and practitioners, the bigger it grew. Although the way the network traditionally sees itself as anarchistic, during the period from 1996/97 to 1999 (which is pretty short in relation to the almost 20-year-old existence of the network) especially the VET & Culture workshops and conferences have become a more conventional style. The first time when this became evident was the conference in Malta in 1996.[6] With it the implementation of a new structural principle of the workshops and conferences has begun.

One year later, the Network was in Norway the first time (1997). The workshop was held in Sørmarka outside Oslo, organized by University Akershus College. People attended from Norway from the University of Oslo, the Work Research Institute, University of Bergen and Tromsø as well as from the employer and labour unions.

The following annual conferences and workshops which were organized by the core group of the network in cooperation with responsible colleagues on different locations as e.g. the University of Bergen (1998), the Swiss Institute for Vocational Education (1999), the University of Bochum (2000) and the University of Erfurt (2002) mainly met certain standards of academic life. In this respect these events corresponded little with the original idea of strengthening the international cooperation in the field of VET research beyond usual pathways.

6 See the last paragraph of section 1 of this chapter.

*Members of the VET & Culture Network*

However, each of these conferences as well as each of the following ones are characterised by presentations and discussions in historical, sociological, comparative, cross-cultural, gender, didactical and methodological and also from learners' perspectives. The common interest of the respective discourses was and still is to point out the productivity and relevance of VET research as a critical comment on global economic, technical, social and educational changes which have taken place in the last decades. The growth of post-Fordist production methods, the implementation of micro-electronics into almost all areas of the working world, the concepts of human capital and employability as examples for new forms of efficiency and other chief influences upon the process towards a substantial change especially in capitalist societies need responses of VET research. In this respect, research in the context of the VET & Culture Network is high lightening the idea to demonstrate both the importance and the power of vocational education as a significant contribution to increase an emancipatory, democratic and empowering education of individuals as an essential condition to their social participation. Thus, the central themes of the conferences and workshops from 1998 to 2002 were:

- "*Economic, Social and Cultural Embeddedness of Vocational Education*", Workshop at the University of Bergen, Norway, August 27-31, 1998.
- "*Gender Perspectives on Education and transnational and historical Lessons*", Workshop 1999 in Aarau, Switzerland, August, 19.-22., 1999.
- "*Lifelong Learning: One Focus – Different Systems*", Conference at the University of Bochum, Germany, August 17.-19., 2000.
- "*Social Competence and Learning: A Relation causing many Questions*", Workshop in Arvidsjaur, Sweden, August 2001.
- "*Marketising and Governance of VET – Driving Forces of Vocational Education*", Conference at the University of Erfurt, Germany, September 19.-21., 2002.

The topics of these conferences reflect the wide range of research in the context of the network. In addition they point to the fact that the discussions which were initiated by the organizers of the conferences are correlating with their expectation to develop new understandings and recommendations concerning the complexity of aspects of society that are labor-related. Furthermore, the presentations and discussions during the sessions of the conferences should lead to further thinking among participants. This approach still is the basis and guideline for all activities of the network.

Regarding some more important matters of the network's activities, the following is to point out: As mentioned above, in the medium term the character of the annual conferences and workshops had developed to a more conventional conference style. This was true for the conference in Malta in 1996, and it had become really evident at the conference in Bochum in 2000. Finally, this event marked the dawn of a new era of conferences. Since then the conferences and workshops have become more international. Especially the conference in Erfurt in 2002 was a first proof of this development. It was the first time that there were participants from outside Europe, Richard Lakes and Patricia Carter came from USA, as well as from Canada. This was followed up in the conference at the labour union conference centre in Sørmarka in Oslo in 2004. Researchers from Africa, Argentina, Australia, Canada, Cuba and the USA met with networkers and other participants from Austria, Denmark, Finland, Sweden, Germany, Norway, Switzerland and UK. The topic in Oslo was "From Hand to Mind. On the Social Organisation of Working and Knowing". Here it was also decided that we should alternate between bigger conferences and smaller workshops every second year.

Another very important matter of network activities was the 10th year's workshop in Mustiala (Finland) in 2003 which was organized by Anja Heikkinen. The central theme was "Occupation and Education in Transition". Beside the fact that this workshop took place at a really nice location, namely at the Mustiala Agricultural College and an elder brewery in its neighbourhood, this conference offered an extra-session of students for the first time in the history of the network's activities.

*Impressions of the VET & Culture 10th Year Conference in Mustiala, June 12-14, 2003*

More precisely, a preconference took place from 10th to 11th June 2003. Looking back to this, one interesting point is that there were presentations amongst others by Maija Vesala from Finland, Gaby Molzberger and Matthias Vonken, both from Germany. Maija is an old timer, but Gaby and Matthias came for the first time. They have been belonging to the steady members of the VET & Culture Network ever since. Another aspect concerning the conference was the public interest in this event. The newspaper article “Ammatti on tärkä osa identiteetti. Kasvatustieteilijät kokoontuvat tällä viikolla Mustialassa” that was published in “Forssan Lenti” on 12.06.2003 by Leena Pärssinen describes both the diversity of the conference programme and the demand of the network on transnational cooperation in the field of VET research in detail.

The following workshop Joensuu in August 2005 included a young researchers conference for the first time. A most important outcome of this conference which was focused on the theme “Transforming Politics in Education and Work” was a paper by Anja Heikkinen and Katrin Kraus on the collaborative research and writing programme for the VET & Culture Network. This paper was the basis for discussions and group work during this workshop. Chiefly, it points out *(a)* some basics of publication projects within the network and *(b)* the thematic areas at the workshop. Concerning the last-mentioned aspect, it also gets clear on which topics the main research in the context of the network in the longer run will be focused:

> “Theme 1. Reconceptualisation of educational and industrial orders (cf. life-long learning employee, open co-ordination); transforming ideologies, discourses and vocabularies – paradigms of education and occupation (division of work) …
>
> – changing patterns/systems of education and occupation (division of work) – agencies, policies, institutions …
>
> – emerging practices and programmes of education and occupation – actors, movements …
>
> Theme 2. Reconfiguration of occupational orders (cf. high-skilled and low-skilled jobs)

> Theme 3. Reconstitution of cross-cultural relations in work, education and research (cf. quality assurance, networking, co-operation, virtuality, multiculturality)
> - historizing
> - contextualizing (comparative, relational)
> - gender-sensitive matters.
>
> The time-frames differ according to the topic (e.g., conceptual reflections may have quite long ones; system characterizations since 19th century; practices/actors 20th century)."[7]

These perspectives of further publication projects and thematic areas are still valid. Nevertheless, in connection with the 13th network conference in Copenhagen in August 2006 a fundamental change became apparent, reinforced during the 14th conference at the University of Konstanz in summer 2007. This conference was organized by Thomas Deissinger. As a result of a longer process of discussing the principles of network activities, the members of the network came to following decision about a structural change concerning the annual network meetings, respectively about the concept of conferences and workshops:

- Each second year a bigger conference as in Bochum (2000), Copenhagen (2006) and Konstanz (2007) shall take place,
- In between there shall be smaller network meetings and workshops.

By that the network reinforced its decision taken to the meeting in Oslo in 2004 to alternate between an open conference (e.g. like Konstanz in 2007) and a smaller meeting like the one in Joensuu in 2005. Thus, a smaller meeting was held in Arvidsjaur, Sweden, from 17th to 20th September 2008. This meeting was organized by Antoni Lindgren, and its character was like a "round table" to summarize the discussion in the network around specific topics, as: Where do we stand? What are the future perspectives? This meeting was limited to 20 – 25 people, but finally just twelve networkers met at this lovely place in Sweden.

---

7 Anja Heikkinen & Katrin Kraus, Information about "Transforming Politics in Education and Work" – collaborative research and writing programme for VE and culture-network 2004-2007/08. Tampere and Zurich 10/05 (unpublished Typescript).

*Arvidsjaur 2008. Close to the location of the meeting*

*A session during the workshop in Arvidsjaur 2008*

*Impressions of the workshop in Arvidsjaur 2008*

The main topic of the workshop in Arvidsjaur was to reflect on fifteen years of VET & Culture Network. In this respect, the following analysis by Liv Mjelde and Richard Daly is quite instructive:

> "From the time that Anja Heikkinen convened the first gathering of European VET researchers in Finland 1993 an abiding concern of the resulting VET & Culture Network has been coming to terms with rapid changes in the linked phenomena of labour market and vocational education and training against an increasingly globalized world. For the past fifteen years, pioneer participants in the network, and others who have since joined, have been concerned with the documentation of what is in reality a set of international phenomena that – in terms of policy, implementation and learning styles – plays out differently in different countries studied, both within Europe and further abroad. (…)
>
> Fifteen years have flown by. The network has been active with annual meetings in August and September each year in various European locations. It now has participants from other continents as well as Europe. It has produced an impressive number of contributed volumes that reflect its annual thematic discussions and debates. (…) In general, the members of the Network have a greater appreciation of one another's national situations, historical trajectories and cultural complexities. But have we managed to move very far along the road of comparative and joint studies in our field? Have we been able to put vivid empirical reality of our local data to work in an internationally significant way? Have we managed to pool resources such that we have contributed significantly to the questions regarding the interface of education, labour market and global trends?
>
> The answer seems to be that while these concerns have been addressed by a great number of participants on the individual basis, and in relation to their own national concerns, the level of collaborative work remains mostly a thing of the future. Granted, a number of researchers have been highly critical and have raised critiques of national VET policy, of ideological uses of VET and its propaganda effects on the workforce, and of the lowly status of VET in comparison with general education. (…)
>
> We would suggest that if the Network wants to develop and grow in a healthy manner, it might benefit from summing up each member's research interests and practices in relation to VET in their country of study, and seek ways of doing this collectively, with a view to building an open and flexible, but common point of view on such questions as
>
> (1) the ever-growing need for conceptual knowledge in VET,
> (2) the low, stigmatized status of VET and VET studies,
> (3) the continued privileging of theory-based higher education over VET education,
> (4) future of vocational pedagogy,
> (5) questions important especially for European VET members, arising from the export of VET knowledge from Europe to other parts of the world – where knowledge from industrial and post-industrial countries becomes exported to the so-called under developing regions. What is worth exporting and what is not?

> (…)
>
> To sum up: What about the growing need for familiarity between Europe and other areas of the globe? In such situations the participants have to be made aware of whose culture, whose values and whose methodological assumptions are being taken up. And which culture, values, viewpoints and methods predominate and become the 'international' medium of social exchange – out in the beyond where Europe sells its educational knowledge and experience – and why certain culture or cultures assume a hegemonic position. And on what basis should researchers from, say North and South, interact for better VET and cultural understanding? How to build the social relations which create the necessary curiosity for doing good international/comparative research? How to enrich critical/cross cultural thinking that can create new and clearer knowledge within the complex field of VET in the future?"[8]

These questions make clear how ambitious the research and collaboration in the context of the VET & Culture Network has been and should be in the future. As another matter of fact, more or less explicitly the questions put by Liv Mjelde and Richard Daly were answered during the following bigger conference in Zurich in 2009 which was organized by Philipp Gonon. The main topic then was "Inclusion and Exclusion in a globalised World". Not going deeper into details, the contributions to the Zurich conference made clear the complexity of problems caused by globalization and pointed out perspectives in the field of VET. Thus, the main focus of research as presented in the sessions is on the following topics:

- Paradigms of VET and their proponents,
- VET as a constituent of life-worlds and life-courses,
- Traditions of learning, teaching and knowledge,
- Economic, social and cultural embeddings of VET,
- Contemporary challenges of VET,
- Contemporary reform policies and practices in the field of VET,
- Administration and politics in the field of VET,
- Connections of theories of VET with the (globalized) world of work.

According to the decision taken during the Konstanz conference, in 2010 there was a smaller network meeting in Hattingen (Germany). This meeting was organized and coordinated by Christina Düsseldorff and Manfred Wahle, and there were two working groups which focused on the following issues:

- Status of the Network,
- Activities in fields of research,

---

8 Liv Mjelde & Richard Daly: Reflections on VET and Culture: Past, Present and Future. Arvidsjaur Workshop, 17-20 September 2008. One Size Fits All? Reflections on Fifteen Years of VET and Culture. Oslo 2008 (unpublished Typescript)

- Collaboration,
- Publishing,
- Concrete work
- Future plans.

As an outstanding result, an "Intellectual Agenda" was designed. This Agenda is shown in the following picture.

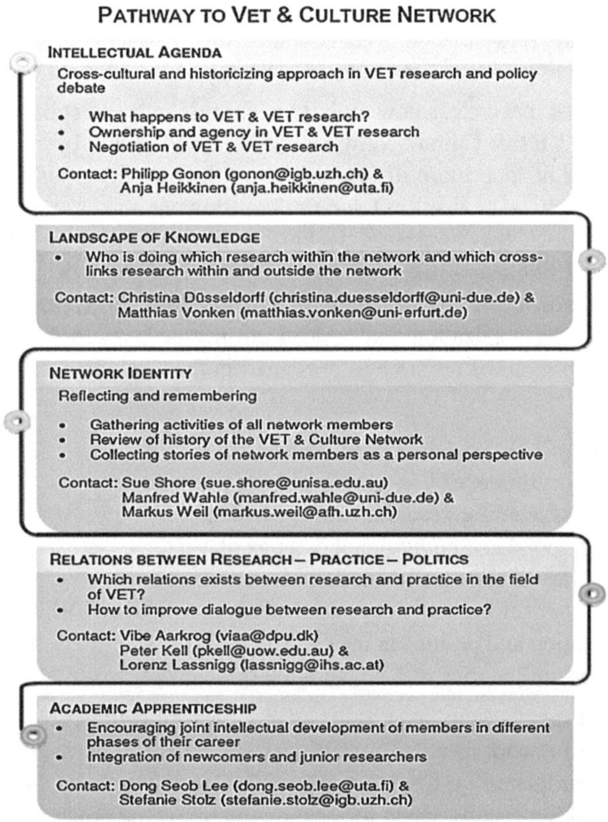


*The 'Intellectual Agenda' of the VET & Culture Network*

In order to execute the Intellectual Agenda, specific tasks, future activities and responsibilities were fixed. This working programme was designed with regard both to the outcomes of the workings groups' sessions and comments referring to these. Though the following activities would not have been finished till the conference in Torino in 2011, some concrete results were taken as important to be presented then:

## Current and future activities of the network (ongoing process)

1. Taking into account the intellectual agenda in future activities: website, meetings, research and study collaboration, publications. Designing a manual for future meetings

The main issue is to make explicit why the network is coming across. In this respect research processes and activities in the fields of VET are central issues. That means to use the opportunities of the network for research and learning proposes (including students activities).

2. Compiling a landscape of knowledge (ongoing process)

Referring to the Intellectual Agenda, a platform of key questions of VET research is to build up. The task is to generate a data base/data file concerning the following aspects:

- Who in the network is doing which research?
- Connections to researchers in the network
- Links to research and projects, mainly inside the network.

3. Reflecting and remembering network identity (ongoing process)

1. Gathering activities of all members of the network: Publications, activities and outcomes of networking
2. Review of the history of the VET & Culture Network
3. Collecting stories of members of the network: the personal perspective.

These stories are based on interviews with different networkers. Their stories shall give information about the following issues:

- Development of the network
- Benefits of networking in a personal perspective
- Personal activities in the network
- Personal demands et cetera on the network.

4. Taking into account academic apprenticeship in all network activities

Developing a pedagogical concept distinctive to network activities, encouraging mutual respect and intellectual development of members in different phase of their research career, one task is to improve the integration of newcomers and junior researchers into the network and its activities.

5. Taking into account relations between research, practice and politics in VET/Connections to practice in all network activities

Which relations exist between research and practice in the fields of VET? How to improve dialogue between research and practice?

The meeting in Hattingen in 2010 generated a lot of perspectives for future activities which are very much related to central ideas in the period of humble beginnings of the VET & Culture Network. However, during the following 18$^{th}$ (and bigger) conference in Torino from 31$^{st}$ August to 3$^{rd}$ September 2011 which was organized in collaboration with the European Training Foundation (ETF) the central issues of the "Intellectual Agenda" were introduced to all participants. There was no doubt that the "Intellectual Agenda" is a really important part of the network's identity, and that it is worthy to fulfil the demands of this agenda. Furthermore the Torino conference was characterized by a lot of papers, presentations and discussions which dealt with different aspects of its central theme: "Research for VET Policy and Practice". Concerning the special character of the conference, that means that the VET & Culture Network came together with the ETF, the following statement of Søren Nielsen from ETF is informative:

> "This conference provides a unique opportunity for researchers to acquire insiders' interpretation of transnational policy processes and for the ETF staff to receive critical feedback on their policy-facilitating approaches. The conference also challenges researchers to confront their approaches and arguments with expectations and imperatives from transnational policy processes. It provides an opportunity for the VET & Culture Network to sharpen its intellectual agenda in asking:
>
> What is happening to VET and VET research?
>
> What is happening to ownership and agency in VET and VET research?
>
> What is happening to negotiations about VET and VET research?"[9]

9 Søren Nielsen: "Research for VET Policy and Practice". 18th VET and Culture Network Conference hosted by the European Training Foundation. 31. August – 3. September 2011. Villa Gualino, Torino. Background Note. Torino 2011 (unpublished Typescript)

*Left: Anja Heikkinen and Søren Nielsen during the Conference in Torino, August 17-September 3, 2011*

*Right: Participants of the Torino conference: not studying the "Intellectual Agenda"*

The quotation above points to the last aspect that is to mention within this review on network activities until the date. Thus, the publications from the network are interesting. By now about twenty common publications are available which include papers presented at workshops and conferences of the network. Each publication offers

- different perspectives on historical, theoretical, didactical and political impacts of the relationship between VET and work,
- provides analyses of historical, recent and contemporary developments in the field of VET,
- each publication documents the arguments and initiatives the network has brought into discussion since 1993.

# Reflections on time and networking

*Rudolf Husemann and Maija Vesala-Husemann*

## First Part: Maija

In order to develop understanding of a phenomenon it is good to have a look to the starting period. A sentence found on my notes made when following the debate and discussion of Anja's dissertation work. These notes, in spite of some turbulent movements of home (library), are still available, and as we – Rudolf and I – got the invitation to contribute to an Anniversary Publication to celebrate Anja's 60th Birthday I scanned the notes through for refreshing my memory and inspiration for ideas and shared them with Rudolf. The dissertation is written in Finnish, like my notes and our discussion happened in a mixture of German and our common Lingua franca English. In spite of the attempt to use only English, we are not able to avoid that this mixture of languages will be visible in the following text. During our discussion three topics emerged: time, network and research on VET.

The first meetings of the network co-ordinated by Anja had started already before her dissertation was published and I as Anja's student had had an opportunity to participate in some of these early meetings. By this time I had already some preliminary understanding of the research interests of Anja. When the date for the defence of the dissertation was agreed, I was very eager to join the public event and listen to the discussion. The public defence of Anja´s doctoral thesis *"Lähtökohtia ammattikasvatuksen kulttuuriseen tarkasteluun. Esimerkkinä suomalaisen ammattikasvatuksen muotoutuminen käsityön ja teollisuuden alalla 1840-1940"*[1] was held in Tampere University on 29th of April in 1995. The opponent, assistant professor Joel Kivirauma from the University of Jyväskylä, made – as the role of the opponent is – questions and remarks on Anjas 501 page dissertation, and demanded answers to and/or clarifications of certain issues. The notes of the situation are subjective and incomplete, nevertheless exciting and interesting to read and reflect for this purpose.

The first theme to focus on – the concept of time – was inspired by one of the first questions asked by the opponent to Anja. The question concerned the following quotation from Egon Friedell's book "Uuden ajan kulttuurihistoria" ("A Cultural History of the Modern Age"). The text describes the meaning of

---

1 Heikkinen, A. 1995: Lähtökohtia ammattikasvatuksen kulttuuriseen tarkasteluun. Starting points for cultural research on vocational education.

time: past, present and future for a human being. The quotation here in Finnish and German:

> "Aika on kenties kaikista kauheuksista, mitkä ihmistä ympäröivät kauheinta: haihtuva ja pelottava, hahmoton ja tutkimaton, kahden uhkaavan epätietoisuuden leikkauspiste: menneisyyden, jota ei enää ole olemassa ja joka siitä huolimatta yhä edelleenkin painostavana ulottuu nykyhetkeemme, ja tulevaisuuden, jota ei vielä ole ja joka kuitenkin jo ahdistavana painostaa tätä päivää; mutta nykyisyyttä emme tajua milloinkaan ... tunnemme itsemme onnellisiksi vain jäsennetyssä, asteisiin jaetussa, välimerkeillä varustetussa maailmassa ..."

Ammattikasvatuksen muutosvaiheiden etsintään sopii ohjeeksi, kuinka

> "on tiettyjä ajankohtia (kuten ihmisen elinkaarella), jolloin uusi ihmislaji syntyy, ei tosin päiviä, mutta ehkä vuosia tai vuosikymmeniä...Uusi aikakausi ei ala, kun suuri sota nousee tai lakkaa, kun voimakas valtiollinen mullistus tapahtuu, kun ratkaiseva alueellinen muutos suoritetaan, vaan sinä hetkenä jolloin uusi ihmislajin muunnos astuu näyttämölle ..."[2]

And the same text in German:

> "Die Zeit ist vielleicht von allen Schrecklichkeiten, die den Menschen umgeben, die schrecklichste: flüchtig und unheimlich, gestaltlos und unergründlich, ein Schnittpunkt zwischen zwei drohenden Ungewissheiten: einer Vergangenheit, die nicht mehr ist und trotzdem noch immer bedrückend in unser Jetzt hineinragt, und einer Zukunft, die noch nicht ist und dennoch bereits beängstigend auf unserem Heute lastet; die Gegenwart aber fassen wir nie...wir fühlen uns nur glücklich in einer artikulierten, gestuften, interpungierten Welt ..."

As an advice to study the periods of changes in vocational education and training fits.

> "... Es gibt bestimmte Zeitpunkte, wo eine neue Art Mensch geboren wird, aber vielleicht Jahre oder doch Jahrzehnte... Eine neue Zeit beginnt nicht, wenn ein großer Krieg anhebt oder aufhört, eine starke politische Umwälzung stattfindet, eine einschneidende territoriale Veränderung sich durchsetzt, sondern in dem Moment, wo eine neue Varietät der Spezies Mensch auf den Plan tritt ..."[3]

*How is this text connected to the topic of the dissertation?* – asked the opponent. In her answer Anja underlined the heuristic meaning of the text. Something new in vocational education doesn't start when a new law or a system appears, but the past includes already the forthcoming new of the future. Egon Friedell's "Zeit" is described dramatically, almost like a personification of "Time" – invisible but present. Something that we want to manage, although at the end it has

2 Friedell, E. 1945: Uuden ajan kulttuurihistoria 1, 76, 79 (cited in A. Heikkinen 1995, 28)
3 Friedell, E, 1947: (18.-21. Auflage) Kulturgeschichte der Neuzeit, 60, 62

the power on us. We will not follow Friedell's (inspiring and exhausting) text further, however the concept of time will be discussed later. In the reflection of the meaning of the time, there are some other heuristic findings, like Fernand Braudel's ideas of time dimensions of structures of culture, and how you can observe different changes: long-lasting, episodic or momentary depending on the phenomenon that is observed (Anja's dissertation page 22). It seems logical to study what kind of changes we can recognize: slow, rapid etc. Slow changes – perhaps another name for continuity – a concept that has helped me through all the years to resist the rhetoric of the permanent need of the rapid changes.

What is then a meaningful change in VET? asked the opponent. E.g., vocational teacherhood, was Anja's answer. In my notes I could see three !!! behind the answer, my own comment to the topic.

In the chapter of the foundation of the aims and methods of the thesis Anja goes deeper into the meaning of cultural, historical and philosophical approaches in research on vocational education. On page 23 she delivers a picture with the title "Kulttuuri, yksilöllinen arvotajunta ja toiminta" (Culture, individual consciousness of values and action). Here I give a draft of the picture, to illustrate the following comment.

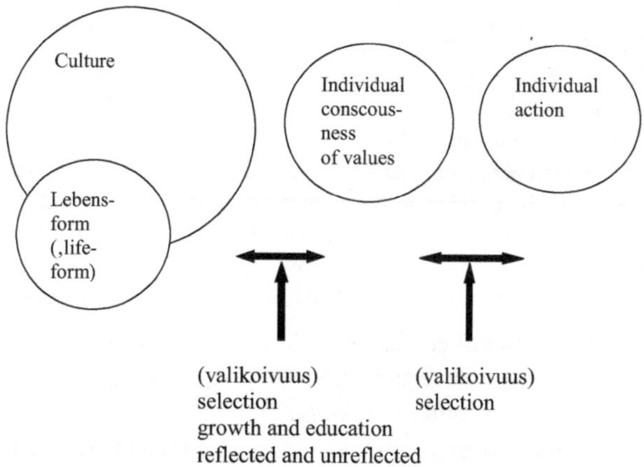


*Culture, individual consciousness of values and action (picture taken from Heikkinen 1995)*

This picture provoked the following question of the opponent: Where is the vocational education in the picture? And later still repeated: is vocational education in the big circle on the left?

It was a thrilling question and still is, indeed, what is vocational education and where is it situated? Is it something in ("objective") culture, is it (intersubjective) in life-form/Lebensform, is it in individual consciousness and/or action? According to my notes Anja answered like this:

Vocational education is in all of them, the picture tries to visualize the complexity of culture, how culture constitutes, what is essential on it. Culture is existing, not loose floating, in connection with lifeforms, and lifeforms are connected with individuals. Individuals are authenticating it all (yksilöt todentavat sitä).

In one of the earlier comments the opponent had asked if the chapter on the foundation of the research methods and aims could be seen as a programmatic declaration? Now – as I found the remark on that – it seems to me that he had hit an important point. Anja was challenging the ways of making research on vocational education "from outside". Using the concepts of life-world (Lebenswelt) and life-form (Lebensform) with full consciousness she committed to make research on vocational education taking the whole "picture" into account. In fact the process was already going on. The research on the peculiarities of Finnish vocational education had already given the voice for the different actors in the field of practice and – as we all know – more was coming. The interaction between researchers and actors in practice is important. The seminar in June 1995 in Hämeenlinna is a good example of it with Anja's own words:

> "The aim of the June-seminar was to experiment and promote ideas from integrating discussion with practitioners, which would benefit both sides. It may require that either research-groups have their own contacts with practitioners or there are parallel networks of practitioners and researchers, before a fruitful international, comparative discussion can be developed. Although neither of those prerequisites was perfectly filled, the encounters with their theoretical, practical and linguistic challenges increased our understanding of complexities and options in developing "research and development"-designs on vocational education and culture in European scale."[4]

The actors of the vocational education field are seen not only as an object of the studies, but the ones who have their own voice and are constituting the culture of vocational education in their own countries.

The "programmatic declaration" also includes a clear part of the role of the researcher in the whole picture. She/he as a researcher is not an "outsider" but an active part of the constitutors of vocational education and research on it. This was also a topic of a comment and discussion concerning another picture (page 19) describing "Todellisuus-aineisto-teoria-kehä" (the circle of lived actuality –

4 Heikkinen, A. ed. 1995: Vocational education and culture - European prospects from theory and practice. 2.

the collected research materials and theory). It is important to reflect what is the role and position of a researcher in the production of the material and hers/his position in the whole, which implies the same that the research is in movement and process in the time-line.

Thus it is natural that also the researchers on vocational education need a platform to change the ideas, share the results and discuss about the differences and peculiarities. Not in the sense of uniforming the research, but benefitting of the variety. To find this kind of platform – in Anja's own expression – she was "forced" to international contacts, and out of these contacts developed a network.

## Second Part: Rudolf

Following Kant's a-priories, our experience and action within the networking is connected to concepts of space and time as preconditions. In the concept of time we can speak about the development of the "growth" and continuity of our network.

"Time" according to the Finnish philosopher G. H. von Wright, "is the escape of human being from the contradiction"[5]. Time – in this sense – can be seen as a concept which gives us the possibility to deal with changes. Our experience puts us in front of demands, tasks and challenges, which we have to reflect about, embed them in our experience and history and let them ripen to action. The network as a social system creates its own time structures, and "future" in this sense is a chiffre for continuity, in German language we might better speak about "Anschlussfähigkeit". Some curious sounding vocabulary around this topic deals with the expression of "progress" or declares the concept of future as something planable, as some technocratic and political positions might try to explain.

What to say about that in the context of networking? One topic of time concepts could be continuity; let´s call it linearity as well, in the meaning of a steadily ongoing process. Another topic could be the curious follow up of past, presence and future, which leaves us inevitably in the moment of the presence although we do not exist without the two other ones. To understand and to be able to make sense of something belongs to this triade. And our reflections about

5 von Wright, G. H. 1968: Time, Chance and Contradiction, Cambridge University Press, zit. nach Nowotny, H. 1989: Eigenzeit - Entstehung und Strukturierung eines Zeitgefühls, Frankfurt, p 52

time should mention something like biography, which could be mentioned as ageing as well.

My first contact to the EUROVET Network happened in 1995, while I was working at the University of Duisburg as a substitute professor for Adult Education. My contribution dealed with changing conditions of VET in Germany after the unification. This historical event had happened five years ago and we had accompanied the following steps of re-establishment with several research projects. "We" was then a group of about 20 scientists which had founded a research group on vocational education in enterprises called “Arbeitsgemeinschaft für Betriebliche Weiterbildung”, the office was located in Bochum. Our knowledge on the subject was actual, political and aware of rapid changes, where we contributed with publications.

The network was pretty young then, some two or three years running. The group of scientists was international but with a core in the Scandinavian countries. The main link to Germany consisted on a good relationship of Anja to the Bochum University Chair of Karlwilhelm Stratmann and his group of researchers on “History of Vocational Education”. Nobody would assume that this focus on history could have been by accident. It might be seen as the core of approaches to the meaning of vocational education “... in times of change ...”, as the network expressed it here and there. So, one of the continuing topics of the network turned out to be history. Of course, the history as a continuing topic had a history as well, which was embedded in an early consensus about a historical and materialistic but as well subjective approach on the observation of changes in vocational education. Historical periods, structural and political reforms, the meaning of vocation and profession in social, political and economic perspectives and how this had found its place in the scientific discussion itself belonged to the subjects of networking over the years.

The other essential concept of the network was “culture” in an international view. The international concept gave obviously a unique idea of difference and variety. This made it possible to widen the networking to any direction and specialisation as well, of which the international comparison was only one. The young network concentrated then on Scandinavian, British and German models and paths of development, but during the years other models were presented and changes in the well known models were under discussion. Aside of the international comparisons, different vocational professions such as hairdressing and teacher education were taken into the focus.

In all these subjects the work of the network had a natural time concept which might be described as breathing or seen in the picture of the tides on the shore of the oceans. On the one hand there were times of preparing conferences, travelling and meetings in certain places in Europe, on the other were times of writing, documentation and reflecting – both carried of the common spirit of understanding and diving deeper into the meanings of work and education for human kind. These breathing times have brought us again and again in front of our computers, but as well to places which otherwise we would never have visited. The places reach from the very north of Europe to the very south. To these places count traditional and modern vocational schools, trade union education centres, private homes, holiday resorts, locations of history and culture and many examples of institutionalised vocational education. In these visits, those places have given us, and we have filled them with, a kind of life which has been one of the unique experiences of this networking. The late summer times when the conferences happened in general gave the possibility to visit local restaurants, eat and drink local products, make boat trips and other excursions, for sports, times in sauna and next to grill fire with long lasting discussions up to the early daylight.

The phenomenological social sciences (e.g. Alfred Schütz and Thomas Luckmann) as well as social theory based on systems and functions (e.g. Niklas Luhmann) had to take up the subject of time[6]. This seems to be unavoidable for the explanation of something like sense (Sinn). And sense is then a meaningful concept, if there were some doubts on causal logics as a general pattern for observing, describing or explaining human action. In the case of a social system like our network, the logical approach would predict something like congruence or identity between members and their view to the subjects of the network. What opens the concept of sense? We can find in it some link between past, present and future which gives us a possibility to locate the individual in a social context. Vocational education and its historical and cultural dimensions have been meaningful to us before we found each other in the network. The scientific life, and may be some practical (biographical) contacts have developed to a topic of a professional scientific career. Of course that means long hours, months and years of disciplined work, especially producing visible results and to distribute them into the scientific community. So the networking works, but in a special way. Sense making in our network means to meet and discuss with a human being - as Liv Mjelde says: "Menschen". Sense making, to declare something meaningful for an own part in social action, means to be seen and respected in a holistic way, in other words, as a unique individual and natural part of the group. The network became a part of our biography.

A biographical concept of time might be understood in a combination of three vertical layers. The middle layer could be seen as the life course itself,

6 Schütz, A./Luckmann, Th. 1979: Strukturen der Lebenswelt Bd. 1, Frankfurt; Luhmann, N. 1984: Soziale Systeme, Frankfurt

from the beginning to the end of life (wherever we locate these forms). This implies that we are equipped with certain kind of body, gender, brains and so on, to be developed and modified within the life span. According to Niklas Luhmann[7] education plays a major role in this process, when he mentions the biography as the medium, which gets shape ("Form") by education.

Above this layer of the life course we locate an area which we might see as the historical and institutional frame of the life course – to be more precise a social frame in a historical change simultaneously to our life span. Aside of the bigger historical trends (economical, social, political) there are the institutions of education, family,employment and what ever a human being gets in touch with. The phenomenological theories would mention this as life world (Lebenswelt).

Under the layer of our life course are our experience and our sense making. In the German education science this layer is closely connected to the idea of "Deutungsmuster"[8]. The concept of "Deutungsmuster" is seen as meaningful for social acting within our biography, as it mentions the combination of an epistemological and an ontological part of our being ("in der Welt sein"). The network has been and is part of this, and acting in it has created meaningful steps and events in the life courses of the members. The biographical idea with its three layers could visualize our being part of the network.

Discussing the networking on the folio of time concepts might give a picture of our own experience being part of it, belonging to our life world. The process itself has been not strictly planned in the sense of a pre-described aim, but rather the development has been an "evolution" when voices of the members have been influencing the way of the network. The remarkable extension and internationalisation of the network, concerning members, topics, projects, publications and meetings, have to be seen as outcomes of the process itself. As participants in the network over some time we have been part of this construction. Along this time, some topics have been continuously on the agenda, as e.g. mentioned the relationships of hands and mind as well as the holistic picture of historical, institutional and subjective perspectives on the development of VET.

---

7 N. Luhmann, N. 1997: Erziehung als Formung des Lebenslaufs, in: Lenzen, D./Luhmann, N. (eds): Bildung und Weiterbildung im Erziehungssystem, Frankfurt

8 Schüßler, I. 2000: Biographisches Lernen, Hohengehren

# Greetings from Lapland!

*Antoni Lindgren*

My first encounter with the VET & Culture Network was at a workshop in Sörmarka, a place nearby Oslo belonging to the Norwegian Confederation of Labour. I had got hold of the invitation by chance, someone had put it in my mail, and it was addressed to the department I still am at: the Department of Human Work Sciences at Luleå University of Technology. The invitation had a somewhat mysterious title: "Work of hands and work of minds in times of change". I believe the invitation came in my hands just before the start of the summer holidays, at the end of June.

At the end of August I was on place, in Oslo. First I went by the public bus and stopped in the forest uphill some mountain and from there I walked in the direction pointed out by a road sign. There was rain in the air so I was happy when I soon saw something down in a small valley that looked as it could be the place where I was heading for. It was a number of squared, yellow bricked buildings spread along the side of a lake. I was relieved, found someone to talk to and I was given a key to a dormitory in a building somewhat downhill. I went outside, downhill following steps in the slope and found my room, which was on the top, on the second floor, on the right with a view facing the forest. Later I discovered that there was an underground pass way connecting most of the buildings, which must be very nice in the wintertime. Somehow, when I am trying to describe Sörmarka I have the feeling that it looks the same as all the other places we have met at; in Hattingen, Erfurt, Arrau, Bochum, Jyväskylä but that is not so, physically but there is the same feeling. It is a feeling of being taken care of, a kind of a family feeling. Someone is taking care of you.

The working principle is that the host of the work-shop provides free lodging etc and you only have to get there somehow. Once you are there, everything is taken care of. I believe there is some broad stairs leading downstairs from the lobby and that the start of the workshop was there, at the end of the stairs. People hurrying, the typical stress/expectation in the air. I can remember only fragments from the work-shop but there must have been many participants, so probably it was more of a conference – the aim is still to alternate between smaller work-shops and bigger conferences. I remember that there was a dinner with many, maybe a hundred gusts and some women, probably a head at the host institution, maybe at Akershus college, at one point was reading Viking poems in English. I had noticed in a bookshop at the Central station – I travelled by train – such a small book. Also I remember I was personally in the lobby warmly welcomed by Liv Mjelde, a voluptuous blond woman, as I learned later a former air-hostess, and by Tove Lien, smiling, seeming to know me from some occasion before. Maybe from some of the Nordic working-life conferences that now had ceased to exist?

Probably there was the usual division between participants; in members of the network having presentations and the others being a public. There probably was some key-note speak with many participants, and then fewer at the many parallel seminars. I have a clear memory of a smaller seminar room and a sort of beginning and welcome – probably there was a network meeting before the beginning of the conference – this was confusing at the first time – maybe a day before. I remember Anja Heikkinen standing up and asking everyone to join in a silent minute memorizing someone from the network. She had tears in her eyes as some of the others as well. It was for Karlwilhelm Stratmann from Bochum, one of the founders of this network, in late 1993, I believe.

Then I understood that this was different from the working-life conferences and workshops I had attended so far. I also understood that Anja is an important person in this network. So small – I almost had to look twice to notice her – with her Finnish up-nose and Finnish English and so full of energy, once let free bubbling over. She reminds me of the forest-spirits she likes to praise. From then on I considered Anja and Liv as the pillars of this network. Another thing I remember was the jogging; some of the male participants in the net-work went jogging before breakfast. This they have continued to do; Håkon Host, Ole Johnny Olsen and Philipp Gonon. This, I believe were the same people, though more people were joining in, among them Katrin Kraus, who have the habit of going for a swim before dinner whenever this is possible.

At Sörmarka there is a lake. I found this a little bit odd, excusing me with that I had brought no bathing trousers. If I remember it correctly Phillip said that this was no problem, adding to my feeling. To this moment I date my conviction that essentially this net-work consists of a bunch of hippies, accommodating to new circumstances. Though I so far haven't joined in the bathing, these people still have changed me in many ways, becoming more flexible. Anja once has told me that her first impression of me was: "Oh NO! A stiff, serious Swede!" I believe that I have become less so, thanks to these warm hearted people!

I do not fully remember who else was there since we met there once more one year later. Apart from those I have mentioned Rudolf Husemann was not there, neither was Maija Vesala or Matthias Vonken. Maybe Manfred Wahle – but not Christina Düsseldorff – was there? Neither Cristine and Madhu Sing, nor Beatrix Niemeyer. Very young ones like Marcus, Stefanie and Antje had not yet joined. Richard Daly was in Canada. Svein Michelsen was not there but maybe Runar Sakslind and Ove Korsness? Those not mentioned not forgotten! Patricia and Richard from the USA had not yet joined. So who else was there? Not Virve Kalioniemi. Not the Australians: Elaine, Sue and Peter. Of course some people have stopped coming, I can still miss them, and some new people joined the network. The most important is that the spirit remains the same. And I believe it will, Anja is the living proof of this. Kiitos! From Lapland!

# From Arvidsjaur to Torino – Mobilising research(ers) on vocational education and culture in an expanding European knowledge society. A personal network story

*Beatrix Niemeyer*

## 1. Setting the scene

I will focus my network story around the idea of travelling. On my flight home from last years' VET & Culture Network's conference in Torino I realised that the number of flights I had done between January and August 2011 equalled the total number of those I had done before my $35^{th}$ birthday. This prompted some reflections about travelling, how the frequency of travelling impacts on social relations and biographical stories, and how dependent the building of the post-modern knowledge society is on rapid means of transport and mobile and flexible individuals.

Research and travelling have always been close relatives. We know about the scholars who travelled the republic of letters in $17^{th}$ century Europe to share the emerging knowledge in natural sciences as well as the philosophic discourse about the individuals' place in the changing world, with Latin as the lingua franca. Another familiar figure from the vocational context is the journeyman, who wandered through Europe to broaden his (or sometimes her) vocational expertise and skills. During the $18^{th}$ century the educational journey became a fashionable habit to broaden the horizons of the sons of the emerging bourgeoisie, demonstrating wealth, educational aspirations and cosmopolitanism and serving the individual desire for discovering new shores or simply being somewhere else. Meanwhile we know about a considerable number of daughters who did the same. As Goethe many of his contemporaries made their way to the Mediterranean sun in the Toscana or to other interesting and inspiring places in Europe. Travelling in these days was risky and exhausting, means of transport were uncomfortable and slow. Travellers needed money, courage and curiosity.

In a certain way travelling always is identity work. It's the process of simultaneously distancing oneself from the familiar context of home, which often is perceived as narrow and approaching new areas, discovering new territories, which seem to be broad and bright, promising new insights as well as new and inspiring experiences. It is not only about exposing oneself to a foreign context and experiencing one's ability to handle uncertainty, insecurity, risks and unknown circumstances; it's also experiencing oneself as being foreign, questioning the own patterns and pillars of belonging. Travelling is broadening horizons, gathering knowledge, learning about oneself and others, and, possibly, to come to a deeper understanding of both the home and the foreign context through comparative reflections. It usually is an inspiring experience.

Today travelling has become easier, faster, more comfortable and common. Changing places of living and/or work has become a frequent biographical challenge. Leaving home has become a common experience, be it for political, economic, social or recreational reasons. Against the calling of global labour markets and the pushing of violent political or social conflicts the subjective need for orientation and stable relationships are easily overlooked. The subjective effects, the biographical impact of this global mobilisation are a marginal discourse only. The art of building and maintaining social relationships today applies new tools. People meet in virtual spaces. Facebook and Skype channel communication from any place in the world at any time. Mobility turns into a character feature of citizens of the flexible knowledge society.

With the mobilisation and flexibilisation of social relations staying connected, getting grounded, slowing down is no longer a yesterday attitude of the conservative and narrow minded, but has become a good of luxury. It was Mark Twain, who said "The more I travel, the better I understand people who stay at home." Orientation, roots and time are precious goods – they are turning into basic educational challenges. The individual's ability to build social relations, to engage into a community, to serve the longing to belong, to actively construct the biographical pathway and to determine on the place and rhythm of living and working are translated into educational tasks. They are challenging research, practice and policy since they are transcending by far the simplified idea of education as transferring and piling up of knowledge and training of competences.

One of the distinctive features of the VET & Culture Network is its sensitivity for this social dimension of (vocational) education. I value it as a social space for orientation, which is at the same time perfectly fitting the conditions of the mobile and flexible globalised knowledge society and critically working against it.

What at the first sight may appear as a report on conference tourism actually is a multidimensional critical reflection on an individual transnational learning process within the liquid framework of the European knowledge society. It reflects the paradoxes and contradictions of transnational research by telling about the irritating and inspiring experiences of doing European research and being an (vocational education) researcher in Europe - and thus may contribute to the ongoing and necessary discourse about the role of the network in the process of building the European knowledge society.

It's like two sides of a coin. Mobility and flexibility need travelling, they build on the process of virtual or physical distancing from the point of departure as a necessary precondition for approaching a new aim, envisaging new horizons – mentally or physically. Reflecting on the politics of travelling, of liberating (knowledge) workers from their narrow home context and train them how to mobilise people, knowledge and competences tells a story about the interrelationship of macro- and micro-level or in other words about the enabling and disturbing effects of a de-territorialised education policy and the arts and politics of connecting people, positioning and safeguarding spaces for self-directed critical reflection.

## 2. Arvidsjaur - getting engaged

My first encounter with the network of vocational education and culture was an irritating one. Travelling through Europe, changing planes in Copenhagen and Stockholm, I finally arrived in the far north of Sweden on a miniature airport in a small town with an almost unpronounceable name - Arvidsjaur. It was of marginal importance during the summer season, but gained a Europe wide importance during winter times, when all prominent car factories came here to conduct their so called 'elk tests'. While I was carrying my usual conference outfit I found myself on the last part of my travel surrounded by Swedish males clothed in dark green on their way to enjoy a fishing and hunting weekend.

On my arrival I learned that the participants of the conference – of the critical and culture sensitive and pacifist network – were lodged in a former military camp which had been turned into a campground type recreation area, close to a lake on the one side yet in walking distance to the local vocational school, which was chosen as conference site on the other. The following days were an uneven mixture of presentations on VET research, self-reflecting discussions on the future of the network and how it should be positioned in the context of European vocational education research and intense experiences of the regional culture.

We were swimming in the lake at morning, enjoying excursions to the wilderness of northern Sweden and a barbecue organised by a Samish couple of reindeer breeders in their tent. The combination of reindeer steaks and red wine symbolised a pan-european cultural encounter, which culminated in the common singing of workers' and folk songs in English, Norwegian, Swedish, Italian and German. On my flight home, surrounded by the former green men now porting a strong smell of campfires, I definitely knew that the VET & Culture Network was different and my engagement would be the beginning of a new type of European experience, working on an own sort of European project - which later on turned into a global one, including a growing number of participants from Australia, Africa and South America.

What was it that made this network meeting and the majority of the following ones different? One reason may be the specific choice of conference sites. For a long time I was convinced that one selection criteria for a meeting place would be that it should be close to a lake (and possibly equipped with a sauna) and a common swim in the morning would belong to the established tradition.

Another thing was the careful composition of the conference program. It provided a specifically balanced mixture of academic discourse and cultural experiences, which gave both elements their own right of existence. The Arvidsjaur conference was a lived experience of simultaneously valuing diverse regional cultural traditions and the people rooted in it. It was a lived way to resist the mobilising and flexibilising politics of the liquid knowledge society, a cross-cultural experience of building a transnational community. It was supported by a special human spirit which was connecting the participants in a way that almost immediately created a sense of belonging. Coffee break talks did not only concentrate on projects, research topics, academic positions and publications, but likewise on biographical stories, outdoor experiences or family backgrounds, in other terms accepting and valuing a balance between work and life.

Another distinctive feature is the way how the theoretical reflection on vocational education is approached. The analysis of the complex relationship of the work of hands and work of minds and its societal consequences transcends the comparably linear attempts to design qualification frameworks for so called less qualified. I appreciated this approach as an enriching expansion of the idea of vocational learning, based on the equity of blue and white collar work. It is valuing work as well as workers through concentrating on the human side of labour relations, placing the human profit before the monetary value of work. This theoretical framework of the network is reflected in the book series "Studies in Vocational and Continuing Education", aiming to "present critical, historical and comparative research", or in the landscape of knowledge on the website. A gender and culture sensitive approach and the prominent role of women also made a refreshing difference to the academic contexts which I had been familiar with so far.

Last but not least the organisational habits also made a difference. The network is not for visitors, but for people who are ready to engage and to contribute to it. All participants are supposed to contribute to the conference, as presenter, discussant or chair of a workshop. The organisation of continuity and change is designed as a collective effort, both enabling and presupposing a collective agency. To summarise: the network for me was and is a space for (self-)reflection of persons who are engaged in European and international research and committed to the European project in a human and political sense.

This perception was confirmed at the following conferences, when we were watching the northern lights in Joensuu, learning about local cultures at a monastery in eastern Finland or at a glass factory in Norway. Another continuum over the years were the regular self-reflective debates, the negotiation about the network's self-positioning in the European research community, where it gradually developed into a well-established factor. The process of institutionalisation was supported by the rhythm of annual meetings, the regular newsletter, and the publication series. The decision to alternate between smaller and bigger conferences was a way to work on the balance between safeguarding a self-determined agenda and the importance to speak into the official discourse of European vocational education research. Interesting enough this went together with a southward move of conference sites, a gradual movement from remote islands for introspection closer to the centre of European research policy.

## 3. Moving on – Torino

In a way the 2011 meeting at the Torino European Training Foundation was the completely opposite in terms of travel experience. Neither walking nor swimming was foreseen on the conference agenda. This meeting however provided a deep insight in European culture of a different kind. In this town of Fiat the history of mobility and mobilisation provided the cultural background – as it was enrolled during a guided tour through the car museum – rather than the local history and personal cultural roots of the local hosts. This time the network conference was located in a virtual European institution with an international community of employed researchers. They are addressing the task of translating the agenda of education politics, which is written in Brussels, into concepts and instruments of vocational/education to be disseminated beyond the boundaries of Europe in a sustainable way. Here it could be observed how the "travelling ideas", which Gita Steiner-Khamsi had mentioned in her key note two years before at the Zurich meeting, are mobilised, when the knowledge workers of the European Training Foundation reported about their planning of VET system reforms to be implemented beyond the borders of the EU, where they meet cultural habits, socioeconomic conditions and human needs as a challenge to be handled in a fair and sustainable way. The VET & Culture Network however, as congregation of experts in critical (self-)reflection was invited to feed back on the Torino process.

## 4. Learning about Europe

As the obvious difference between Torino and Arvidsjaur illustrates the contexts, tasks and topics of research on vocational education in Europe and the world have shifted – not only for the network. The magic triangle of research, policy and practice is gaining an evidence which covers the illegible system of power of which it is constructed. Paradoxes and contradictions, dilemmas and disturbances, asynchronies and uncertainties go along with reconfigurations and transformations of the re-construction of this specific interrelationship.

The differences between the Arvidsjaur and the Torino conference, the distance between the two cities in a way signify the tensions going along with it, and they highlight the way how the network positions itself in the centre of the according discourse. And again the practice of travelling conceptualised as the contemporaneous process of distancing and approaching may be crucial to allow for a change of perspective and enable critical reflection on just some of the following complex questions or topics.

*Mobility as a mindset*

While a couple of decades ago travelling abroad could be considered as a positive indicator of being open minded and – especially against the background of the racist fascist period in German history – as an expression of the need for international understanding, today we find it on the top list of educational targets. It has become a general educational aim. The Erasmus program for example is directed at mobilising the next generation of Europeans, literally. It is encouraging and funding learning and working experiences abroad. Mobility however, seems to have turned into an end in itself, into a training program to become ready to leave the home country to work and live anywhere else on the globe. In this perspective mobility programs appear as a strategy to free individuals from their established boundaries of their national contexts of home and the social communities. Yet individual mobility may well go along with enriching and inspiring personal travel experiences. These implicit and non formal processes of learning are hard to be arranged and hard to be assessed. It is possible to count the number of countries travelled or of flight miles, but it is much more complex to evidence-base the related experiences of uprooting or alienation or the broadening of horizons and the strengthening experiences of self-efficacy which necessarily go along with travel experiences of an individual.

### *Standardisations and singularities*

The growing of Europe comes along with processes of standardisation. Money, language, products, life-stiles, topics, policies and practices in welfare and education are gradually aligning. The capitals of the nation states are adapting their outside appearance. Global chains of food, clothing or furniture companies settle all over the world, making the big cities as well as their inhabitants uniform – and, by the way, devaluing vocational learning. English is developing into the lingua franca, in almost any member state it is coexisting and amalgamating with the national languages. At the same time those normative orientations which have been developed together with the national projects of welfare states are still effective. The unification and standardisation of working, living, learning and consuming does not dissolve national habits, orientations and peculiarities at the same time and at the same speed. The mediation of a "same but different" and "different but equal" Europe remains a challenging aim for educational efforts on both the political and the practical level.

### *Comparisons and competitions*

Transnational comparisons are a proved and established heuristic instrument. In an international context research processes are inevitably connected with comparisons. The question why some things are different and what exactly is different, what could be the reason for these differences and how they could be explained, is a process of learning which goes along with a better understanding of the other as well as of the own context. Comparisons need equal categories and differing features. "You can't compare apples with pears", as an old German proverb says. Yet, if categories and features are adapting and amalgamating, comparative research comes to limits. At the same time comparisons gain importance in policy making – the PISA contest illustrates a milestone in this political turn of the focus on figures and evidence. On their way from research to policy comparisons turn into competition, so that the improvement of statistics and the amelioration of figures are privileged over the understanding of the social conditions which have produced them.

The meeting and matching of top-down and bottom-up movements again is challenging research and practice. Top-down strategies building on outcome-orientation are directed at the improvement of the evidence provided by benchmarks and indicators which have to abstract from national, regional, local characteristics. Simultaneously bottom-up movements of people joining in common activities, engaging in meaningful practices and caring for common concerns could follow a completely different agenda.

## 5. Concluding Remarks

This list of topics could be extended; more could be said about the re-territorialisation of the social for example, or about the flexibilisation of vocational education, about the ownership of knowledge, etc. Furthermore the reconfigurations of the complex relation between work of hand and work of minds remains a challenge for educational policy and practice and a persistent task of VET research.

Against this background the network provides a space for research and reflection. It is sustaining the right to put the own questions on the research agenda and to reflect the own (personal and collective) involvement into the European process. With a critical perspective on standardizing, unifying, marketising processes in European education and VET research it has established a discourse which acknowledges and explicates individual and collective cultural roots thus aiming at a deeper understanding of cultural diversity within Europe and the world. Network meetings provide the frame, the space and the opportunity to reflect on a personal and collective research agenda, which has not been imposed by funding schemes and governmental research programs. Therefore they are both: a territory to be safeguarded as a re-action against mainstreaming research policies, a space for identity work, and a time-out for critical reflection. They provide the necessary space for orientation and connectedness in the liquid modernity of the EU knowledge society – they are a political territory and a space for policy at the same time.

# Invisible fortunes of cross-cultural higher education. Three untold stories about an ERASMUS teaching staff exchange

*Markus Weil*

## Introductory remark

This article deals with a teaching staff exchange from October 21st to December 4th 2006. Due to its personal nature it is written in "non-polished English". The main purpose of such a use of English in a non-English speaking environment is effective communication and not a native speaker imitation (see Mauranen et al. 2010, Weil/Pullin 2011). For the occasion of writing this book chapter the use of English in the function of a lingua franca might be appropriate. In the teaching context itself the use of English as a lingua franca in higher education has been broadly researched, mainly from the perspective of applied linguistics (see e.g. Frankenberg-Garcia et al. 2011).

## Prologue (story 1)

Kalevankankaan hautausmaa
Once I stood in your snow
What was hugging me to your ground?
That's, what I don't know

I have heard from sisu many times
But never could I see
That it's not you, not you my dear
It's your sound and melody

Where stones by stones stand on the yard
That was not of my cue
My thoughts were taking me up high
Where you taste like joulutorttu

Viinikankatu, Kalevantie
You sound like wood and sea
Once I stood there freezing in the snow
I felt you faithfully

## Corpus (story 2)

*Introduction*

Some things stay invisible. Does this mean they are non-existent? A whole tribe of philosophers and an army of theologians and even natural scientists have dealt with this question. But also on a day-to-day level within academia we can ask ourselves about the invisible – often untold – fortunes of what we are experiencing in our university environment. Or the other way around: Do we only take for granted of this academia what is visible? Why do important and fortunate thoughts have to be written down, writings be published, publications be registered, registers be compared in order to be taken into account? Visibility has become a question of accountancy and effectiveness – higher education is no exception of that. What Husemann and Heikkinen have formulated for vocational and continuing education appears also more than true for higher education: "Now commitment to EU and globally most competitive economical areas has challenged [… the historically grown relations]." (see Husemann/Heikkinen 2004, p. 1)

This article highlights an experience only few people at the time have had the chance (or interest) to take a look at.[1] Possibly because the experience has not claimed to be of economic value and not geared at global interests – and yet it might be an expierience of a cross-cultural higher education similar to many situations in our university environment. It could be shared, compared, ideas could be developed further and cross-cultural teaching and learning settings could be advanced beyond the rethorics of mobility and a European Higher Education Era (see e.g. EHEA 2011). Still this experience is not labelled as proper research because the data collection was not scientifically founded, neither as proper teaching because it was not a right part of the curriculum; and neither as proper administrative procedure, because it was not a strategic focus of the participating universities. So even in the "third space-discussion" of projects between and among administration and academia (see Whitchurch 2008) it cannot be nicely located on either side or as a third-space project inbetween, because participating lecurers have been part of all three areas at the same time. Neither it might be visible or countable for that reason. In opposition one could argue that this experience demonstrates that an academic community always consists of a research approach (including towards the own academic work) and critical thinking, that cross-cultural experiences are part of our university lifes and do not necessarily fit into a curriculum and that

1 The formal request of documentation was a one-page report to the international office of the home university. A presentation about the lecturer's perspective on the exchange is accessible online (in German, see Weil 2009).

administration is part of that process, too. Instead of continuing mouning, here is an attempt to make visible, discussable and sharable an experience from a teaching staff exchange in 2006 in the module "Made in Europe – European Qualification and Quality Frameworks in Education and Training" at the Unviversity of Tampere, Finland (see Made in Europe 2011). This is an example of cross-cultural higher education very much in favour of the activities of the VET & Culture Network like the EU Curriculum Development Programme Crosslife (see Crosslife 2011), annual network meetings or the Trans-national Qualification Framework (TQF) seminars (see TQF 2011). And this cross-cultural higher education teaching experiment existed, even though it was not very visible.

*Information about the teaching staff exchange*

Part of the teaching staff exchange was the module "Made in Europe – European Qualification and Quality Frameworks in Education and Training", consisting of a course with 15 participants from nine countries including three distant students from Australia, Switzerland and Malta[2]. The teaching staff exchange was based on an eight-week visit from Markus Weil (at the time University of Zurich, Institute for Upper Secondary and Vocational Education) to Professor Anja Heikkinen (at the time University of Tampere, Department of Education).[3] The aim of the module was to grasp the concepts and different levels of quality assessment within the education system as being related in a socio-cultural way (see Made in Europe 2011). Furthermore the module description reads: "The course starts with the identification of definitions concerning the main concepts education, quality and effectiveness. These concepts have different connotations from the students' background, on an institutional or on EU-level. Further on small groups will develop own scales of quality criteria for education in a certain setting and compare this to criteria and aims given in EU papers. The differences and similarities show the mentioned levels (students, institutional, EU) in a practical setting of comparing and developing quality criteria for education." (ibid.) The participating students were asked to formulate research perspectives in a practical field and to look whether or not and how the concepts were used.

2 These students were follwing the course on a learning environment and occasionally during video conferences.

3 The Department of Education at the University of Tampere as well as the Institute of Upper Secondary and Vocational Education at the University of Zurich have witnessed reforms, fusions and re-namings after 2006.

*Teaching Diary*

During the visit I have been writing down the experiences and reflections including a range of site visits, the teaching and preparatory work as well as attendance to staff meetings etc.[4] This diary is one form of data that can be used for further reflections and developments. It might not be called research data, but it is supporting a research-approach towards university teaching by observation and self-reflection (see about using a teaching portfolio for these purposes Futter 2009). The sections of the diary presented here are about the teaching experience following the lesson plan of the module "Made in Europe – European Qualification and Quality Frameworks in Education and Training". The writings are selected, extracted and reflected from a hand written diary filled-in (nearly) every evening. Why to publish such personal, subjective and narrative material? That is part of the answer to the question, whether things only exist when they are written down: They exist for the people who have been part of it without writing it down – but for all others they only start existing now, when you are reading about it. Also Anja Heikkinen's encouragement to use self-reflection and the own rationale as a data source for academic or critical thinking, development of concepts and theories as well as putting incidents in a historising context led to the decision to share this experience in order to compare, discuss, reflect on and inspire further developments in our universities cross-culturally.

*31. October 2006*: Reflecting on the course I think it was a good start all in all. I realise (and did so already at my home university) that co-teaching takes more preparation work than doing it alone. We are actually not dividing our workload, but put some coordination tasks on top of it. These processes should be taken into consideration when planning modules and programs in an inter-cultural setting. It is necessary to negotiate, explain and adjust the teaching plans with the co-teacher and additionally explain the previous experiences and the different cultural contexts.

During the course the technical aspect was taking over at the beginning. This might be typical for inter-cultural settings, too. We wanted a video camera to identify the places where to get it and to whom to speak to took longer in the unfamiliar environment. I was organising administrative matters in another language and context, the languages not matching to each other (the administrative environment was Finnish-speaking but mostly communicating with me in English, which is not my mother tongue or my mind set either). In terms of the technical settings I wanted to try out a new camera to have the chance to learn how it

4 In the teaching diary I will use the personalised form „I" as the „genre" of this part is a diary

works and operate it on my own. I think if you are teaching alone this is not possible at all, because you have to concentrate on the course.

We used PowerPoint presentations, overhead slides and the camera for recording the session. Beside the presentation about the topic of quality and effectiveness within education (see also Levin/McEwan 2000). We organised small groups for discussions. This quite complex situation led to the unforeseen: We forgot some of the basics when teaching. We created confusions with the place and the time, even if the rooms have been settled and the time has been planned properly. To be honest, I do not like these time plans anyway, but they seem the only way to keep in mind what needs to be done – and I need to remember writing down the basic information each time even if I know it, but I might forget it when other things are taking over.

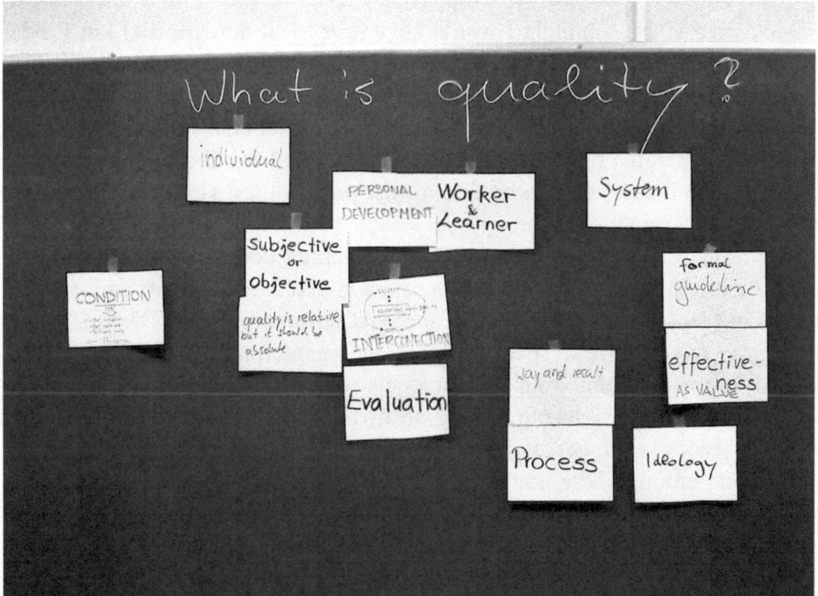


*Picture 1: Taken during the first course day on October 31st 2006*

In my opinion we created a good atmosphere among the participants coming from all these different countries. There have been some cancellations by students, maybe due to the fact that the course is only voluntary. But I know what it is like from my own experience as a student. After having introduced ourselves and having outlined the course we continued with the question "What is quality?" We asked students to write down their answers (1-5 words) on cards.

I really like starting with these cards and the small group work. It makes everybody talk and it gives a picture from the group (also from its cultural diversity). What we did not manage because of mistaken time planning is connecting the cards to some theoretical input. Still the first discussion afterwards was very good as we discovered the different approaches towards quality and effectiveness. But when the course program was discussed in more detail there was again confusion about the research task for the students – still the discussion around this was exactly about the intended topic. I think some confusion is good for the start to get your mind fresh and alert. It seems a rule that the best discussions often cannot be recorded – the camera was off during this part of the course.

*7. November 2006*: I thought I would have time to sit down earlier but I didn't. So this is the reflection on the second session, which took place already three days ago. The course went well again from my perspective. But it is extremely exhausting because I had to follow the content of the conversation in a foreign language, I operated the camera (video and pictures) for documentary purposes and of course I also had to negotiate further proceedings with my colleague and the students during the course.

I still stick to the principle to write a planning document for each session. We hit the important issues during the session and agreed silently on what will be left out or who is taking care of the next unforeseen part. The small group work gave us a chance to speak shortly how we interpret the situation and how we will proceed. In the groups the students were discussing various quality approaches. I think they began feeling an ownership of the small-scale research projects and it is even necessary to tell them not to overexpand their task. There is only one group, where not having a certain threshold level of English might be a problem for one group member. One other student is challenging the organisation rather than the content ("I want to join another group"). Anyhow I think the presentations and group work are a good way to make the students know what is their own decision what they have to do. And they will have to document and reflect on their research agenda.

The web-space offers an appropriate outline for the sessions. However, until now there has been only one discussion thread in the online forum. It seems difficult to establish an online discussion culture, but it is crucial for the three distant students as they don't have many possibilities for interaction otherwise. The work with one of the distant students is intensive. The student cannot access some files on the web and it is difficult to find a solution around it. The technical support in Tampere is very helpful: They transfer files and give suggestions for feasibility with all that technical equipment. But they charge.

This diary seems to be a burden for me. But I feel that I must write because in my mind the impressions will be fading very soon and also others don't have access later to what was happening. Also I think it is better to use these diaries for the later recommendations and reflections rather than only counting on one's memory. But it feels like useless work at the moment.

*14. November 2006*: This time the small groups were different again. We had one complete group and the others were lacking members for several reasons. The main points this time were giving some conceptual inputs and on the other hand developing the small group work plans. We created a break two times when students could relate their topics to the input of governance from distance and trust. I think the input was very well demonstrating the backbone for the research projects.

The students' faces this time seemed to look more serious and tired. I hope it is not because of us teachers. I explained the method of observation during the small field research projects and about the work plan as part of the methodology. The second half of the session again was group work. One of the local students had put some information on the discussion forum in the virtual learning environment and one distant student answered during the course in a videoconference. That was initiating the online forum, because in my opinion it showed the use of it. And I am very pleased that it has been used largely since then. Two groups will already have some presentations soon. The students on the one hand seem to be very keen to go to the field of practice in order to do research but on the other hand it seems a bit overwhelming for them. Also we must not forget the theoretical input beside the practical field studies.

*21. November 2006*: I continue reflecting about the sense of reflections. Again it is already two days after the course and I force myself to sit down and write something. I can describe how the course was, but it is not so clear for me what is the point about it. I also should find out more about structural things, but there was not much time for preparation, so the conclusions would not be very prosperous.

One small group presented their results this day. The process was very narrative, which is fine for the beginning but I hope there can be also a focussed view on the quality and effectiveness (or other explained topics). In the second half my co-teacher made a presentation about the history of the Finnish education system, which was useful for contextualizing the impressions from the field.

But again I do not know if it represents the long bow to quality and effectiveness as a topic of the course.

I would need some time to look at the documents myself. On the other hand it depends on the function of the teacher. I am not teaching in that sense. I see that I am a moderator. But then – what does a moderator have to know? Is he part of the learning process or just moderating it for others? Anyhow I took the chance to do some practical work as well and went to the polytechnic with one of the student groups. That was a good experience for me, maybe I would even formulate that as a recommendation: To go to the field together and include the senior staff. I think at that moment the course came into life also for me and it was interesting at the same time to look at the students and how they try to get hold of certain information.

*28. November 2006*: Today we had three small-group presentations. It was again challenging to operate the camera while teaching, plus the videoconference with one distant student simultaneously. I think the discussion via video is easier with practical issues like the field reports than with theoretical discussions. During the videoconference with the virtual student it became clear that there is not much sense in showing written material into the camera without sending and preparing this beforehand. The advantage of the video connection is the good use for communication. Although I think it is not easy to concentrate very long and the time while one person is talking should be rather short. The presentations have shown that the students have been very active. Some of them have been compensating if others didn't communicate. I am annoyed by the fact, that absence is not discussed. E.g. some students only told me that they will be away without any further comments. I think this should be told to the whole group. And I also think there must be a minimum attendance and negotiations, how the small groups can work if somebody disappears for a while. On the other hand what can the group members do, if one other member says before, that he or she will not come? Absence should be combined with the offer to read or comment online and that there is some reliability. We didn't spend very much time during the planning and I was not keen on giving many rules, now it seems we have to take things as they come.

*5. December 2006*: I had a videoconference with the students and the co-teacher. I was in Zurich, they were in Tampere. I tried to comment all papers and progress in the online discussion beforehand and I think the groups are proceeding on their own. The videoconference went well also technically. Compared with the earlier videoconferences it was much easier access and good sound and video quality. Also all participants were used to this kind of setting. My role was to comment on the group presentations and to "be visible" in that sense that I am still there. I think a video connection is much more vital than with written communication and it can work well with students and teachers being at different places.

*12. December 2006*: This time we had a videoconference both teachers in Zurich and all students in Tampere.

In advance I thought this would be the most challenging part of the course, to speak to the students while we are not physically there. But it went much better than I thought. The connection to each other is not as clear as in face-to-face contact but it is still a good possibility to have personal contact. The groups talked about their reports and then we had a "round table": Everybody should say what the comments for the other groups are. This slipped to a personal feedback and went slightly into the direction of the evaluation that was planned in a written way.

*Picture 2: Videoconference in Zurich with students in Tampere.*

After the break we could connect to that and ask for personal feedback as well. We used the picture of the question “What is quality?” from the first session. And it was striking to me that some of the students still knew what the discussions about a certain topic have been. So I think for some of the students it was good to have that connection to the first lesson and it helped to fresh up the memories and reflections on the personal development.

*Preliminary conclusion*

In the teaching diary mainly four different themes were highlighted frequently: (1) the planning and administration of the cross-cultural course, (2) the course syllabus and learning aims, (3) the communicative aspects face-to-face, with media support and in terms of language and (4) the role of reflecting the own teaching experience. This might not be innovative or new, but anyhow these four areas widen the view beyond a cross-cultural course that only needs mobility and then everything is done. They make visible also aspects of cross-cultural higher education that are not part of political or institutional agendas. Neither these aspects seem to be developed systematically for the curricular or didactical discussions. This preliminary conclusion from the teaching staff exchange example follows the four mentioned areas with the means of making visible and shareable what we have experienced in a cross-cultural higher education setting.

(1) *Planning and administration*. Not only the group of students and the co-teachers were from different cultural backgrounds in terms of origin, disciplinary culture and experience, also in the planning and administrating processes the exchange situation broke up routines and questioned the self-evident within the new university environment. In terms of planning, time has been always an issue, because the assumptions from the home university have been challenged by the intercultural setting: Processes took longer than expected. More negotiations had to be made for the course proceedings. Co-teaching and media use added-up to the time frame.

I think the workload for the students was already at the top end of what to expect. I have experienced the planning documents for each course day and for the overall course as helpful for keeping the rough outlines, but we never stuck to the plans as soon as they have been agreed on. This flexibility seems to be crucial for the setting because on the one hand a program is needed as an outline, on the other hand time should be used flexible and as a resource for reaching the learning aims.

(2) *Syllabus and learning aims*. All in all in the course the theoretical content was limited by time restrictions: there was no time to reflect *together* on the

books and written material. The module was focussed on the field research. For the future I would try to integrate more text reading and especially put attention to the reliability that texts have been read. I have the impression that most of the students have learnt something about the content of quality and effectiveness within education and they will remember it because it is connected to a field visit and discussions in the sessions.

In the self-reflections of us teachers we discussed the use of certain didactic elements like the picture of the question "What is quality?". We came to the conclusion that it is very beneficial to make visible the different views in a group and relate them to the different cultural backgrounds, where the students are and what they bring into the group. It also makes everybody say something – and that is important in order to share, discuss and compare ideas.

For the small field research projects it was very important to build ownership within the small groups. In some groups it worked better than in others it might be worth thinking about ways of fostering that process from an intercultural perspective. All in all the students did much more in these small projects than expected.

(3) *Communication, media support and language*. The intense use of media seems only possible in a co-teaching setting and/or with intensive technical support. The video-conferences with the distant students during the sessions and later also with teachers have been a suitable way to connect cross-cultural perspectives more lively and include different views. Furthermore the online learning environment, which was used in a more interactive way after a few sessions, helped to make visible the different perspectives and cultural contexts. For example all participants were asked to introduce themselves and to read the other introductions. This was a good start to make students reflect on their own position within the course. For me it was very intensive to concentrate on media and on the content at the same time. There needs to be a first face-to-face-introduction to create a feeling of trust to each other before using the online tools. Also the role of media was important for documenting the process.

(4) *Sense of reflection*. The course brought for me a very new dimension as a university teacher, which is concerning the parallel processes in the intercultural setting. Firstly I was preparing the content of the course, as a second task I was exploring the technical equipment and tried to fit it to the content (video material, texts, pictures, video-conferences). The third element for me was the co-teaching, which meant tacitly negotiating during the whole session. These three elements of teaching integrated into each other. I was very tired at the end of each session but I think it was beneficial, because it was not limiting

knowledge to reading a book. I would appreciate very much to share and develop that experience regularly; I think it is an opportunity for international teaching environments in higher education.

In the diary I was often asking the question if it is really necessary to sit down and write. After nearly six years, my answer is “yes”, because not writing down means to leave the experiences invisible. Of course I still remember some incidents and feelings during the exchange, but now I can look at the teaching diary as data that allows me to reflect further from a more distant position and try to (re-)contextualise the cross-cultural experience within higher education. It even is possible to make this process visible with authentic material, which I hope is inspiring discussions and shared developments within university teaching.

## Epilogue (story 3)

This article on the invisible fortunes of cross-cultural higher education ends with an anecdote about a picture. When I was arriving at the Department of Education at University of Tampere for the teaching staff exchange in 2006 there was a poster with all members of the department including name and picture. All but a few: Also Anja Heikkinen’s picture was missing. So I put up a picture from a previous teaching staff exchange in Zurich. I would like to show this here: Only because a person is not visible, does not mean that this person is not there!

*Picture 3: Taken November 12th 2005 during a teaching staff exchange in Zurich.*

## *References*

*Internet Sources:*

Crosslife (accessed 30.11.2011).
http://peda.net/veraja/uta/vetculture/academic_apprenticeship/crosslife
EHEA (accessed 30.11.2011). http://www.ehea.info
Made in Europe (accessed 30.11.2011).
http://peda.net/veraja/uta/vetculture/academic_apprenticeship/madeineurope.
TQF (accessed 30.11.2011).
http://www.peda.net/veraja/uta/vetculture/conferencesandevents/conferences/tqf.

*Other Sources:*

Frankenberg-Garcia, A./Flowerdew, L./Aston, G. (eds) (2011). New Trends in Corpora and Language Learning. London: Continuum International Publishing Group.

Futter, Katrin (2009). Das Lehrportfolio als Dokumentationsmöglichkeit und Qualitätsnachweis in Hochschulen. In: Beiträge zur Lehrerbildung, 27(1), pp. 74–80.

Levin, H.M./McEwan, P.J. (2000). Cost Effectiveness Analysis: methods and application. Thousand Oaks: Sage, 2. ed.

Heikkinen, A. (2004). Methodology: Culturally embedded actor-based approach to gendered core competences. In: European Commission (ed). EU research on social sciences and humanities: Gender and qualification. Luxembourg. Office for Official Publications of EU, pp. 37–47.

Husemann, R./Heikkinen, A. (2004). Preface. In: Husemann, R./Heikkinen, A. (eds). Gover nance and Marketisation in Vocational and Continuing Education. Frankfurt a. M.: Peter Lang, pp. 1–10.

Mauranen, A./Hymninen, N./Ranta, E. (2010). English as an academic lingua franca. The ELFA project. In: English for Specific Purposes, 29, pp. 183–190.

Weil, M. (2009). Internationalisierung der Lehre „And then was chaos all over the place..." Dozieren im internationalen Kontext. Dokumentation eines Lernprozesses. Presentation at the University of Zurich, Center for University Teaching and Learning, 18. November 2009. Available online: https://cast.switch.ch/vod/clips/280fa65pdq/link_box.

Weil, M. (2011). Internationalisierung der Hochschullehre - rehabilitiert? In: Weil, M./ Schiefner, M./Eugster, B./Futter, K. (eds) Aktionsfelder der Hochschuldidaktik. Von der Weiterbildung zum Diskurs. Waxmann: Münster, pp. 251–279.

Weil, M./Pullin, P. (2011). Teaching in English. Didaktische Konsequenzen in der internationalen Hochschullehre. In: Berendt, B./Voss, H.-P./Wildt, J. (eds). Neues Handbuch Hochschullehre. Berlin: Raabe Verlag, pp. 1–20.

Weil, M./Stolz, S./Otazo, P./Baumgartner, E. (2010). Academic apprenticeship in cross-cultural settings: Impacts on university teaching and learning. In: Korhonen, V. (ed). Cross-cultural Lifelong Learning. Tampere: Tampere University Press, pp. 207–224.

Whitchurch, C. (2008). Shifting Identities and Blurring Boundaries: the Emergence of Third Space Professionals in UK Higher Education. In: Higher Education Quarterly. 62(4), pp. 377–396.

# 'As tears go by…': Changin' views on the relations between research, practice and politics

*Lorenz Lassnigg*

This contribution reflects on how the author has changed his views about the relationships in the triangle between research, practice and politics through the years he collaborated with Anja, which are the most part of his working life. The views were always somehow different, as Anja has been always more critical, whereas the author has tended to be more of a 'believer', at least towards certain aspects, and being critical to others. Anja's preoccupation was always with culture, whereas this concept was for a long time more or less outside of his attention, considered as a somehow unclear concept, being more of private than of professional interest for him. The author's preoccupation was always with politics, and with the possibilities of research to influence politics, or rather policies, in a positive way, making it more rational and more just, or at least more equitable.

The title should signal some regret, and also some retreat. The first spontaneous idea has been 'as times go by'. Then, soon the memory of the title and the melancholic mood of the song by the Rolling Stones 'As Tears Go By' came up. It should mean that in the past there had been tears about what could not have been achieved, however, these tears have 'gone by' somehow, because the originally desired achievements may finally turn out as being unrealistic anyway, deserving no tears any more but rather reflection. As a next step the author realised that he did not know what the meaning of the song should be and what the title should express, and he looked into the internet. The text of the song does not increase clarity – it is really lyrics. Interestingly a story appears that Jagger and Richards would have originally texted 'as times go by', and their manager Oldham would have changed 'times' by 'tears', so it's a kind of patchwork lyrics, and a real coincidence too; maybe this stories can inform us somehow how culture works.

## Opening up towards Europe

The first project during which we came in touch was called EUROPROF 'New Forms of Education of Professionals in Vocational Education and Training', a two years EU Leonardo da Vinci Project.[1] The first meeting took place now over fifteen years ago in April 1996 in a really old production site for sponges from the sea that has been transformed into a gorgeous hotel and meeting centre at the island of Hydra in Greece. The aims of the project were expressed as follows:

> 'The long term aim of the project is to develop a 'community' of VET researchers and practitioners and the 'professionalisation' of VET, in other words to gain the recognition of VET as a discipline and a profession in its own right. In the shorter term the project aims to build an international network of VET researchers and to develop new qualifications for VET professionals, planners, teachers and trainers, through a European Masters (MA) qualification to be offered in universities in different European countries.' (Project website, home)

The project had eight 'cornerstones', which turn out very ambitious until today:

1. anthropocentric production supported by 'shaping skills': workers should be given the skills and the autonomy to shape and control technology in the production process and to design and control work organisations
2. developing social innovation
3. social inclusion
4. VET to become recognised as a discipline
5. professionalising VET professionals through university based education programmes
6. need for a new occupational profile for VET and HRD professionals
7. a new curriculum for VET and HRD combining pedagogy with technical and vocational knowledge and work based skills
8. project methodologies based on the concept of collaborative research through an action research approach bringing together research and developmental traditions.

With respect to the understanding of policy making, i.e. of how the cornerstones could feed into practice, the project did not have a deliberate position, and – besides – a European Master for VET does not seem to exist until today (in the internet we can find European Masters of Educational Management, of Adult Education, even an organisation called European Masters for Skilled Crafts, which, however, is a kind of consultancy for implementation of European policies in Oslo).

A key tension in the project has been between the ambitious (utopian) approach of professionalization according to the 'shaping principle' which in fact has set out to change the whole enterprise culture as well as the attitudes of employees towards their working environment in the European capitalist economy through the education of VET professionals on the one hand, and the reception and adoption of the professionalising strategies focused towards the Human Re-

1 A small website about the project is still available: http://www.itb.uni-bremen.de/projekte/europrof/default.htm

source Development (HRD) profession by the ASTD (American Society for Training and Development)[2] in the United States on the other hand, which rather aims at the strengthening of the HRD profession within capitalist corporations around the world.[3] The latter has been supported by quantitative surveys in some European countries about the structures of the HRD-profession, and the basic ideological divide was also paralleled by methodological differences related to a quantitative 'positivistic' approach vs. the qualitative orientation towards collaborative action research.

Both Austria and Finland were new member states to the EU at these times, and the author and Anja have taken very different attitudes to this accession process, which resulted in quite different positions taken in the project towards the relationship of research, practice and politics. The experience of the author was rooted in more or less technocratic oriented policy related research about education and employment, and in particular evaluation of labour market policies. The impact and improvement of policies towards reasonable and equitable objectives has been the main mission of this research, and some networking existed with medium level officials in the labour, education, and science ministries who held similar orientations. The EU membership has at these times strongly reinforced these ideas, and brought several additional sources of expertise into the Austrian scene, but has also changed the basic conditions of policy making, as the scope for economic and fiscal policies has been limited for Austria. There were quite polarised debates about these questions, and the author took a very positive position towards the EU and worked also as an expert in the field of the evaluation

2 See http://www.astd.org/ASTD/aboutus/; ASTD is not only an US organisation but tries to organise HRD professionals on a global scale: 'ASTD International works with International Partners to develop and support a global community for learning and HRD professionals. The ASTD International Partner program provides partnership options including ASTD Press, Education Program, International Delegations, Membership, and Regional Events.' (http://www.astd.org/membership/international/Inter nationalpartnerlist.htm) Partners are shown in Brazil, Canada, China, Japan, Korea, Saudi Arabia, Singapore, Spain/Mexico/Argentina, South Africa, Taiwan, and also in some European countries: Denmark, Netherlands, Spain, United Kingdom.

3 'At the 1946 convention, ASTD adopted a constitution that set as its goals: to raise the standards and prestige of the industrial training profession and to further the professional's education and development. Those goals have remained part of ASTD's mission, even as the profession evolved and needs changed. (…) In recent years, ASTD has widened its focus to connect learning and performance to measurable results. In 2000, the organization chose to refer to itself just by the letters ASTD, to recognize that the profession looks far beyond training in its quest to 'create a world that works better.'' (http://www.astd.org/ASTD/aboutus/history.htm)

of labour market and – the then beginning – of lifelong learning policies supported by the European Social Funds (ESF). Despite the critique of the neoliberal drive of the EU the policies and the modes of policy making in the respective fields seemed a progress as compared to the previous Austrian practices, which the author had experienced for about ten to fifteen years in various policy related research and development projects, the progress appeared in particular:

- the quite strong rhetoric towards equity and social inclusion, which has supported at these times positions rather at the margin of the political spectrum in Austria
- the project oriented and at first sight more effective approach towards policy making, which included much more research and 'rational' arguments, as compared to the strongly politicised and demagogic style of debates in Austria
- the broadening and elaboration of the materials brought into consideration by the EU-documents, which have related the research community much more strongly to the international scene.

Thus in these times the attitude of the author towards the opportunities for an improvement of practices in the triangle of research, practice and politics has been quite optimistic, with the EU being perceived as an ally towards improvement. The basic intellectual frame was quite old-fashioned, simple and naïve (influenced by Carol Weiss' position towards evaluation, Peter Wagner's position towards the impact of research through reform coalitions, and Harold Wilensky's strong emphasis on the importance of implementation): Policy making can and should improve (the conditions of) practice and research can and should help in this endeavour by providing material for a more 'enlightened' way of policy making. Practice itself, however, was (implicitly) taken as a kind of black box in this frame, with the proposition that policy would know too little about practice and therefore would need to be better informed, in order to provide better conditions for practice (a core idea of 'evidence based policy'). Another more silent proposition has been that practice would need policy for improvement.

On this background the involvement in EUROPROF was led by a more general interest in the possibilities of professionalization to improve education, and in the possibilities of policy to shape the professions, without having a background in working with these professions. The clash between the utopian shaping approach and the positivistic HRD-approach was not resolvable by the author; somehow it went straight through him, having sympathy for the need for a change in the approach towards working in the capitalist economy (which, besides, seemed somehow not so completely unrealistic at these times before the millennium, when the optimistic views of Post-Fordism have set high expectations in the 'new economy'), and also for a more pragmatic approach towards improvement of HRD within the enterprise sector and the 'positivistic' acquisition of knowledge about these practices. The result was a more or less descriptive mapping of the VET and HRD profession in Austria.

Anja's approach appeared somehow completely opposite at various dimensions. First her background originated from practice ('*In my pre-full-time-academic life I have worked as a mathematics and science teacher and teacher-trainer in gymnasium and vocational college, as head of local board of education and in educational planning.*'); second, in research she worked in the academic environment of the university in educational departments; third, her view of the relationship between education and policy making was oriented towards professional autonomy, seeing politics rather as an interfering than as an improving entity, and seeing research as a support to practice; fourth, her perspective towards Europe was much more distant and sceptical, perceiving the economic missions as dominating issue, and the domestic politicians and bureaucrats building a kind of coalition with the EU in order to somehow 'Europeanize' the whole community according to similar artificial 'systemic' standards of managerialism (the term '*Busnocracy*'[4] is denoting these relationships); fifth, her research was oriented by a clear mission towards the analysis of how culture holds together the different domains of society and produces them somehow, and the use of qualitative and historical methodologies to perform this analyses; finally, her attempts to transnational cooperation in research were always really focused to transcend traditional academic habits of (narcisstic) presentations and confrontations of ready products towards approaches of *real* collaborative activities, attempts that very often proved difficult for the author (and probably also others being stuck in the traditional habits), but in the end has led to an impressive body of publications.

If we try to relate Anja's approach to the triangle of research, practice and politics, we find that research should defend and support practice against assaults from policy, and deconstruct the abstract and universal images processed in the policy discourses by tracing them back to the time and space of when and where their representations happened, doing this in a reflexive way by being aware that researchers themselves contribute to reality by producing these images (see Heikkinen 2004[5] as an example of her reasoning).

---

4 If the term is typed into google, we can see that Anja has some practical copyright on it, as 42 hits from various countries come up which lead to publications of her, or references to them [search 12.1.2012].

5 Heikkinen, Anja, 2004: Models, paradigms or cultures of vocational education. European Journal of Vocational Training, No. 32 Mai - August 2004/II.

By contrasting the two positions we can see how differently the relationships in the triangle can be conceptualised. Anja's contribution to EUROPROF was an analysis of how vocational teachers' conceptions of their practices have changed in Finland (Heikkinen 1997),[6] as compared to a kind of structural analysis of different types of VET and HRD professionals in Austria by the author. Anja's message was and still is pointing to the direction, that a systematic streamlining of profiles would lead to an impoverishment of the diversity of local practices, whereas the author showed a generalised change from 'old' types of professionals in VET with segmented profiles and high division of labour to 'new' types in HRD with much more holistic profiles.

## The innovation hope

Another collaboration has taken place under the COST (European Cooperation in Science and Technology) Programme between 1997 and 2002 under the heading of 'Flexibility, Transferability, Mobility as Targets of Vocational Education and Training' (see Achtenhagen, Coffield and Evaluationsteam 2003).[7] This broad project covered in five working groups the whole range of VET from context and inputs through processes to output, evaluation and assessment and included some most important and powerful researchers from 16 countries; it supported only the direct costs of networking mainly through workshops. It has lead to several publications, some directly under the project umbrella,[8] others outside in the academic community (Achtenhagen, Coffield and Evaluationsteam 2003, 25-26). Anja and the author contributed to working group four termed somewhat mysteriously 'initial conditions', which produced an edited volume about issues of flexibility (Nijhof, Heikkinen and Nieuwenhuis 2003).[9] Anja served as co-editor, and she and the author contributed chapters in the section 'Professional

6 Heikkinen, Anja, 1997: Education or Training? Changes in Vocational Teachers' Conceptions of Their Work. Cam- bridge Journal of Education 27, 3, 405-23 (http://www.itb.uni-bremen.de/projekte/europrof/docu/doc_3.doc).

7 See http://www.cost.eu/domains_actions/isch/Actions/A11; Achtenhagen, Coffield and Evaluationsteam, 2003: in Neue Wirtschaftspädagogische Forschungs- und Entwicklungsarbeiten, ed. Frank Achtenhagen, Göttingen (http://www.wipaed.wiso.uni-goettingen.de/as/downloads/Band28.pdf).

8 http://www.cost.eu/library/publications?pub-domain=0&pub-year=*&pub-action=A11

9 Nijhof, Wim. J.; Heikkinen, Anja; Nieuwenhuis, Loek F.M. (Eds) 2003; Shaping Flexibility in Vocational Education and Training. Institutional, Curricular and Professional Conditions. Dordrecht: Kluwer.

Conditions' about problems of professionalization (Heikkinen 2003; Lassnigg 2003),[10] which either somehow continued the work done during EUROPROF.

The COST experience included two outstanding issues with respect to the relationship of research, practice and politics, first it was a highly political project that reflected the rhetoric about necessary change and innovation at the edge of the millennium, second the working style was strongly determined by a push towards 'excellence' of the publication plans and a climate of competition of being accepted as 'excellent'. The overall structure of the project was based on the rationale that VET research should explore as comprehensive and detailed as necessary the conditions for the promotion of flexibility, mobility and transferability of VET systems. Based on a feasibility study, a mapping of the concepts and the dimensions involved for the achievement of these goals had been provided during the first phase of the project, on which the subsequent research should build (Nijhof, Kieft and van Woerkom 2001).[11]

The mapping study deliberately proposed to use a broad European research community to structure the whole field of VET towards certain generalised directions by using a systemic approach, and thus to give a strong and concerted impetus to 'produce reality'. In fact the project attempted exactly to achieve, what Anja has critically analysed as the role of researchers in her historical research (Heikkinen 2004), and she was part of the undertaking. Consequently she tried to bring a reflective turn into the activities, which was somehow a hopeless fight against a group of men eager to exert influence by an excellent publication – around the meetings of the working group the author remembers the fiercest debates with Anja about fundamental political questions of the development of the economy and society. Finally the book included for each section a critical review by an external reviewer (Leif Hommen on institutional and organisational flexibility; Fernando Marhuenda about educational tools, and Phil Hodkinson about professionalism), in order to bring a reflective element into the undertaking; this must be attributed as a merit to the editorial effort of Anja.

It is not possible here to evaluate the impact of the project on the structuring of VET policies and systems in Europe. We must consider that it took place around the times of the Lisbon Summit which has substantially increased the European activities in education policy by applying the 'Open Method of Coordination' also to education. The subsequently developed European Education

10 Heikkinen, Anja, 2003: Transforming VET policies and professionalism: a view from Finland; Lassnigg, Lorenz, 2003: Professionalism as a path for the reform of VET systems.

11 Nijhof, Wim. J., Kieft, Marjolein, van Woerkom, Marianne, 2001: Reviewing flexibility; a systems approach to VET. Luxembourg: Office for official publications of the European Communities.

and Training 2010 Strategy has also developed a quite comprehensive mapping of education and training policy (EU-COM 2008; EU-COUNCIL 2001), which still serves as a kind of blueprint for education and training policy.[12]

At this time the author was very much impressed by the promises of the 'innovation hype' in the discourse about Post-Fordism and the New Economy, in particular by the approaches of innovation system by Bengt-Åke Lundvall and his collaborators, which were presented as a kind of 'win-win'-alternative to neo-liberalism. In short, innovation should contribute to economic growth which is necessary for prosperity in capitalism, thus policy should support innovation being flanked by distributional policies against exclusion, and education serves as a main contributor to innovation. Because innovation needs continuous learning the education system must be developed towards lifelong learning. In the sphere of work a turn towards innovation would mean more involvement of workers, reduction of the division of labour, flat hierarchies and better use of competences and qualifications (the expression of the 'high skills equilibrium' has denoted these expectations) – in short a kind of optimistic and utopian view of economic and societal development which, however, had as its precondition quite fundamental changes in politics away from competitive strategies using low wages and cost cutting towards the support of innovation and lifelong learning. Because strong economic interests were interpreted in this direction, this change should be possible, and was combined with a kind of 'third way' attitude towards politics. Of course, this was not seen as a wide and smooth avenue, but a try to changes in this direction was deemed worthwhile. Superficially this approach also fitted well into the Lisbon strategy, which used a similar rhetoric about innovation.

In terms of the triangle of research, practice and politics, the approach mentioned above was reinforced. Research should be brought forward by the analysis of practice along the innovation paradigm, and policy should be informed about how this path can be supported and implemented. There was a fundamental difference between Austria and Finland at these times, as Austria was very traditional in terms of innovation (there is much research available which proves this, and currently there is also a consensus in the policy field that innovation activities should be substantially strengthened), whereas Finland was seen at the forefront – so there were big tasks in Austria to do. Consequently the author

12 EU-COM Education and Culture, 2008: 'Education & Training 2010'. Main policy initiatives and outputs in education and training since the year 2000. http://ec.europa.eu/education/policies/2010/doc/compendium 05_en.pdf; EU-COUNCIL, 2001: The concrete future objectives of education and training systems. Report from the Education Council to the European Council, 5980/01 LIMITE EDUC 23, Brussels, 14 February 2001. http://ec.europa.eu/education/policies/2010/doc/rep_fut_obj_en.pdf

took an advocacy position[13] in favour of analysing and working out the implications of a consequent innovation strategy for education policy, in particular exploring the lifelong learning paradigm and what should follow from it for Austrian education policy.

Within the COST project the contribution was focused on the question whether professionalization can be expected to be a reasonable path towards reform in education. The answer was negative because the exploration showed that the attitudes of professionals must be expected to depend strongly on their self interest and on the shape of the system and the policies taken: if the system and policy is conservative, the professionals will also tend to be conservative. Despite the different approaches towards professionals, this result somehow coincided with the results of Anja's contribution, which also showed a strong influence of the (political) environment on the VET professionals in Finland.

## Clash of cultures

In parallel to the COST project another network of VET researchers has been funded by the Fourth Framework programme (FP4) of the EU between 1998 and 2001, the 'FORUM for European Research in Vocational Education and Training'.[14] The official aim of this project was directly related to the support of the 'knowledge based society':

> Aim a) 'The 'knowledge based society' as a European path for economic development. The European Commission poses a specific European path for economic development which stresses the centrality of human capital to a high skills- high value added production paradigm in a 'knowledge based society'. Europe can utilise the cultural diversity and richness of social and historical traditions to develop a socially

13 To show how hard this undertaking was in Austria the author remembers two reinforcing key experiences: The first refers to a high level group of the Social-Democratic Party (SPÖ) that debated the development of a new programme for education; the author tried to make strong arguments for the support of innovation which had been left out in the draft; the answer by one of the members (a university professor who later became the science spokesman of the green party) which was uncontested by the other members of the group was: why should we push towards innovation, this is a topic from the others (he meant the conservative party ÖVP) anyway; the other occurred in the internal presentation of the results of a big task force within the 'future lab' of the SPÖ for the innovation of the public sector to the then Austrian chancellor from the SPÖ; after the presentation he leaned back, stretched his arms behind his neck, and said: this is very interesting and reasonable, however, it would mean that we need less people in the public service, and the consequence would be an increase of unemployment which we cannot want.

14 http://www.itb.uni-bremen.de/projekte/forum/Forum_framesets.htm

> based innovation culture. Vocational education and training is central to the vision of a socially based innovation culture. It provides the basic skills, knowledge and technical abilities required by an industrial and scientific culture to support the work process, to develop a culture of sustainable innovation and the creation of employment opportunity.'[15]

This network included some thirty partners from 18 countries which should develop transnational research. Five broad topics were selected that structured the work and organised the interested researchers: cultures, values and meanings; labour market; institutions; learning organisations; identity formation. The network met twice a year in different locations for in total nine workshops that were organised according to the five topics and provided a good opportunity for the building of contacts and co-operations among the partners. This worked out well, as previous relationships from the EUROPROF project were reinforced, and some partners formed later the nucleus of the VETNET in the European Educational Research Association (EERA), one of the most active networks. Anja was co-leading the culture group, whereas the author started as a member of the labour market group, and was selected later as a leader of this group.

The author tried to develop an integrative conceptual framework of how the co-ordination of education and employment might work in contemporary capitalist societies. This framework was strongly oriented to medium level co-ordinating mechanisms (bureaucracy, market, associations, networks), and their interrelationships. The basic idea was that the assumptions about simple and straightforward mechanisms which underlie policy making cannot work because of the complex relationships of interacting coordination mechanisms in real systems. Policy was not addressed directly in this framework. An underlying idea was that neither the traditional ideas of bureaucratic planning nor the contemporary ideas of the market as the all-encompassing alternative could work as co-ordinating mechanisms, but new policies must be found that take into account the more elaborate self-organising mechanisms among the actors, in particular networking. The main emphasis was not on policy proposals but on deconstructing and understanding the complex relationships from an underlying innovation policy approach. The idea of informing policy making by research remained alive in this activity.

Addressing the triangle, two issues stand out. First, the network implicitly included the disciplinary tensions between pedagogy and social sciences, as well as the thematic irritations caused by the 'cultural turn' in the human and social sciences, by which the 'cultures, values and meanings' group was driven. Unfortunately these tensions were not made explicit, and no meta level was estab-

15 http://www.itb.uni-bremen.de/projekte/forum/Forum_framesets.htm: > Aims

lished to discuss them – so the intentions by the culture group to question the simplistic ideas of the 'knowledge based society' underlying the project appeared continuously as an irritating criticism of the constructive intentions of informing policy making; as pedagogy has much more in common with a 'culturalist view' than the social sciences, there appeared some competition to a (positivistic) social science perspective, and the author learned very much later more about these issues. The second big issue concerned the question of how transnational research should be developed, and in particular what collaborative research could mean. The funding was provided for the travel and the meetings. So the spontaneous practice of the partners was to bring their research into the workshops, exchange ideas, results and methodologies, and to try to produce some publications. Collaborative research would mean, however, not only to bring together existing things, but rather to produce something new out of the network – this attempt proved too difficult.

In retrospect an important question for the author is how the professional practice in the triangle of research, practice and politics was related to the practical development of politics in his country. In 2000, in parallel to the Lisbon summit, the Austrian government changed from a coalition between Social Democrats (SPÖ) and Conservatives (ÖVP) to a new coalition that included the populist right wing party (FPÖ) which had won the second most votes in the election, with the Conservatives (ÖVP) who led this government. As is generally known the Austrian president as well as the EU have initially unsuccessfully tried to interfere against the new government. In fact education policy changed not substantially; the minister remained the same, and got additionally the responsibility for science and higher education as the ministries were merged. The main public officials responsible for schools and universities, the most important of which were Social Democrats, also remained the same. The change agenda of the new government was targeted mainly to the destruction of the corporatist modes of governance and, in particular on the disempowerment of the labour movement and the oppositional Social Democratic Party. In education the rhetoric changed strongly towards issues of 'quality improvement', 'outcome orientation', and 'new governance' according to ideas of New Public Management – in fact a strengthening of what Anja meant by 'Busnocracy'. However, at the practice level not much has changed in schools, albeit the university has undergone a radical reform towards autnomy – paradoxically this reform was moderated and supported by the longer term Social Democratic director general.

The author acted somehow schizophrenic as he stuck to the previous agenda of trying to inform policy, notwithstanding the different political orientation of the new government. The European and international policies could be taken as some anchor point a fortiori. PISA 2000 was an important event, showing quite mediocre results that were in strong contrast to high expenditure for education as compared to other countries. The search for the improvement of quality became a common agenda in Austrian research and policy; only very few researchers decided to resist a co-operation with the new government. Populism and the fight against it appeared and still appears as the main practical political agenda, and the two established political parties of the traditional conservative vs. social democratic spectre did and do not find a receipt against it, except becoming populist themselves. An important element of this development was that it hid and disguised in fact the appearance of neoliberal policies. Superficially there were no signs of a real neoliberal policy; on the opposite, some liberalisation and rationalisation of the traditional and conservative Austrian structures seemed welcome and necessary to improve education.

## ‘Evidence based policy and practice?’

Rather late the author joined the main international activity of Anja, the ‘VET & Culture Network’, not least because he was employed in a non-university environment and had to earn money through funded research. ‘VET and culture’ exists now since 1993 and is a long living and largely unfunded and academically very productive network that produced among others the Peter Lang series ‘*Studies in Vocational and Continuing Education*’ co-edited by Anja. The first participation in a network meeting (in Oslo) was a very strong experience because of the co-operative and non-competitive climate the author had never experienced before at a similar event. Somehow it was the participation in this network that made the efforts by Anja in the other projects much more understandable.

The Torino conference of the network addressed directly the issues of the relationship between research, practice and policy, and it was very instructive because it was organised jointly with the European Training Foundation (ETF) and combined two cultures, the critical academic culture of the network and the applied policy oriented culture of the ETF.[16] Becoming older, the author has in the meantime accumulated more experience in more direct involvement in policy making and accordingly more tight relationships with policy makers. Milestones were the involvement in events of the Austrian EU presidency 2006, the contribution in a broader consortium for the development of the Austrian NQF, the

16 An article based on the author’s key note to this conference has been published: Lassnigg, L. 'Use of current best evidence': Promises and illusions, limitations and contradictions in the triangle of research, policy and practice. International Journal of Training Research 2012, Vol. 10, No. 3: 179–203.

involvement in a high level Task force about school reform in Austria appointed by the new Social Democratic minister of education, and the participation in a task force for the development of an Austrian Lifelong learning strategy. These experiences allowed somehow for a personal testing of the ideas about the relationships between research, practice and policy, and they led to quite severe changes of the perspectives and assumptions held previously. We can sum up the changes by a kind of late 'cultural turn' by the author, and the insight of the severe limits of 'evidence based policy' posed by the practice of policy making, as well as by the limitations from research itself.

- A first basic personal misunderstanding concerns the previously assumed curiosity and demand for enlightenment from the side of policy makers about the complexities in the field concerned, i.e. education. In the abstract one can of course better influence and shape education the better the complexities of the field are understood; however, given the constraints of time and space and the need for taking decisions, there are rather prefigured beliefs than open curiosity. Therefore a debate has come up about a different kind of research needed for informing policy, as compared to academic research ('evidence based policy research') that has to follow certain criteria, e.g. timeliness, brevity, focus to their questions. The big question about this is, whether this separation in fact leads to different results and accordingly different messages from the different kinds of research. The somewhat tricky and cynical slogan of 'policy based evidence' should indicate that policy would select the kind of evidence from the available variety that fits best to the current interests. Summing up, there seem to be different logics from research and policy which might be brought to the formula that research is bringing up ever new questions about what seems clear, however, policy wants answers and tends to reject questions. As a consequence, the policies are often already clear, when research comes into play; the author experienced this in at least two of his policy involvements (NQF and school reform).[17]
- A second point concerns the understanding of politics and policy making, in particular the question of how policy is related to practice in the triangle. Here we have two contrasting paradigms that make a big difference for the potential impact of research: a hierarchical relationship with a more or less straightforward impact of politics on education vs. a systemic view that sees

17 Shortly after the constituting session of the task force for school reform, at a stage of a brainstorming about the aims and agenda, the members (and several other persons) have received an email with a formal proposal for an amendment to the laws about schooling including a new organisation of school structure, without having been informed about this idea.

politics as a system in its own right situated at the same level as the other subsystems of society without a direct influence on them. According to the latter paradigm the functioning of politics is guided by the aim of the preservation of power and the maximation of votes, which is different from the best possible governance of other subsystems, e.g., education. In this case research provided for politics supports policy practice rather than educational practice. The author had to learn during the years that against his previous belief the latter view seems to fit better to reality.

– A third point is that the ideas developed from the research side about good policy proposals tend to differ in kind from the policy proposals that are feasible for the side of policy making. The main issue here is complexity vs. simplicity. A typical example in Austrian education policy is the topic of financing. There is a strong consensus that 'good' policies for education must mean to spend more money, therefore better quality means more money; consequently the debate is focused on the question of spending more money or not, other things are too complicated. In particular, policy cannot really cope with the problem, if education is already too expensive. Another related point is that in order to maximize votes simple messages must be brought through the media and messages also must survive the competition with the other parties. This is not easily possible with complex policy proposals. A recent attempt to influence Austrian education policy by a referendum for broad reform has with much effort won about 6% of the electorate, absolute 380.000 signatures; compared to 1,2 Mio students (parents) at school and about 200.000 students in higher education entitled to vote the signatures represent about one in four interested persons.[18]

If we relate these issues to the triangle of research, practice and policy the distinction of policy and practice becomes very marked. The triangle literally shows two different paths out from research, one to policy, and one to practice. The original map has been to provide research to policy to improve practice. The revised map says that we cannot assume that policy will improve practice, we even can put into question whether it is able to this if it is willing. Research for policy and research for practice are different things, and the relationships must

18 If we estimate the sum of these figures for parents of children and young people at school plus students in higher education, both have been called for support by important representatives about one in four of those 'directly interested' persons have signed; a referendum asking to amend the welfare state [2002] into the constitution has won about 12% of the electorate in times of the right wing government; around these times previous referendums for the improvement of education policy [1989 and 2001] have won about 3-4% of the electorate.

be established differently. Somehow this is what the cultural approach always was striving for. Questioning the 'Busnocracy' would mean to analyse policy from the perspective of practice, instead of doing the opposite, evaluating practice for the sake of better policy. So the author had to go a long way to arrive where Anja has already been long before.

# Transitions as an educational problem

*Philipp Gonon*

## Introduction: The phenomenon of transition in the educational sector

The memorandum on lifelong-learning issued by the commission of the European Union says that "the successful transition to a knowledge-based economy and society needs to be accompanied by an orientation toward lifelong-learning" (European Union 2000, p. 3). Therefore, new basic qualifications such as computer literacy, entrepreneurship, foreign languages and social skills are required. Epoch-making turns are characterized as transitions when they apparently change society fundamentally, and they usually concern all members of a society. This is why learning seems necessary since society changes toward becoming a knowledge-society which is a gradual not a sudden development.

Also the OECD talks about transitions: "Making transitions work" is the programmatic subtitle of the study "From Initial Education to Working Life" (2000). "Übergänge", "transitions" and the French "transitions" deal with the transition from school to the world of work. It is in particular the – said in an old-fashioned way – contrast between school and life which requires a bridging and is therefore called transition. The vocational education sector has well provided for making these transitions easier: "Manual Work" as a school subject, work-based subjects at vocational training schools, and also the "third learning place" besides school and business. This "third learning place" is introductory seminars which allow for the learning of practical skills in a secure and organized school-like environment. One part of educational research has been concerned with so-called "Employment-Research" for the previous years. This branch establishes the professional development of young people after they have finished school or their vocational training.

Transitions are times which allow for a stepping from one place to another and also from one status to another, possibly higher, status. Transitions are designed to help with this change of place or status, to simplify and to ensure them. They do not allow for continued remaining, a neither-nor for a prolonged stretch of time such as for instance Anna Seghers describes in her novel "Transit". She recounts how the protagonist provides herself with a visa for transit, a "Visa de sortie", which allows the immediate departure to another country in order to be able to remain inside the occupied France of the Second World War.

Only the documentation of the stage of transit provides her with the long hoped-for prolonged residence permit.

"Rites de passage" play an important role in times of status transitions. Transitions are coupled with work and trouble They often prove to be not entirely unproblematic with regards to the individual, their organisation and society which is why they are highlighted by special stagings. The first day of school is sweetened for a child by a special present of sweets or little nick-nacks, the celebration of the Abitur (A-level equivalent) rounds of the time at the "Gymnasium" and the "baptizing" or "gautschen" of book printers (pushing an apprentice into a well) following the completion of the practical examination marks the end of the status as an apprentice and the welcoming into the profession's gild.

These important transitions are also marked by examinations and are documented by certificates which are a kind of "entitlement": The "Matura" entitles its holder to study at a university: at the age of 18, a driver's licence can be acquired and the self-steered driving – not learning – may start.

Transitions are not only important when changing from school to the world of work, but also from family to school-system and, we may add, between the different stages at school. This is the case because transitions also need to be completed when returning to school from work in order to later return to the world of work as in the case of those re-employed. Transitions into the educational system and into working are nothing singular when closely looking at it: the course through the educational system may be regarded as a sequence of transitions.

The reason for a transition is, first of all, the transition itself and its successful completion. Transitions as establishments or institutions regulate the furtherance from a starting-point to a clearly defined goal which is easier to reach via the transition. But transitions also play an important role in terms of time. One of their central features is the gradual change that is a slow, as opposed to an abrupt, turn. This is why the ripening of a fruit and also of the human life may be perceived as a sequence of transitions.

Also in this regard, it can be stated that a goal is defined by managing transitions, one after the other and successively, for instance to age while retaining one's dignity. Nevertheless, transitions can occur in unplanned or unwished ways: for instance the transition from soberness to being drunk in the sense of mentally slipping away, but also the transition from a full-time job into unemployment. Especially in order to make individual temporal transitions easier, society has created structural transitions. Transitions therefore include a structural and temporal dimension. In order to make transitions from healthiness into frailty more bearable for the elderly, and also for society, a whole armada of social workers and social education workers is busy with ensuring transitional structures. Also the transition from childhood to adolescence is cushioned by a number of small transitions. It is supported by a great number of people and institutions who are involved in this transition. Transitions from school to the world of work overlap with the transition from childhood into adolescence or post-adolescence.

Generally, also transitions themselves are describable as temporal and therefore chains of transitions. The transition into the world of work looks different today from 30 years ago, and the above mentioned report by the OECD states that the times of schooling have been prolonged successively. A certain minimum of "upper secondary education" is nearly universally obligatory which causes problems especially for those young people who are tired of school and wish to leave the school system early, since they are nevertheless exposed to a temporally prolonged schooling. Transitions are consequently in transition which is especially the case when the transition into the world of work is delayed, the aim is unclear or the transition even loses its outline altogether.

We have mainly referred to a structural and temporal dimension which is defined by the bringing together of two places and/or conditions which are defined as distinct from each other. This is the particularity of transitions, the overlapping of individual and structural elements and the latter are to be counted as temporal transitions in themselves. What I will be proposing in the following paper is an education and an educational theory under the perspective of transition – which is often used merely as a technical term. Transitions are then parts of transitions, they make larger transitions easier and are themselves in transition.

## Learning as a sequence of transitions or: What little Hans doesn't learn, Hans won't learn either

Learning, no matter whether it is lifelong or not, is considered to be a second degree change by learning-theorists. The tension between a current starting point and a modified state at a later stage can therefore be understood as being part of the problem of transition. In my view, this is very well documented in German sayings which demonstrate a difference between *not yet* and *but then* in a folksy way, for instance in "Too much is unhealthy" (Allzu viel ist ungesund). The publication "Die Erziehungsweisheit im Sprichwort" (Educational wisdom and sayings, Metzler 1953) links this also with a too much in terms of compulsory learning in schools. *Those acting like a donkey have to carry the bags* (Wer sich zum Esel macht, muss Säcke tragen). The following saying directly refers to our topic here: *Those getting lost on their way to school also won't find their way through life* (Wer sich auf dem Schulwege verirrt, findet sich durchs ganze Leben nicht zu recht). The prime example of sayings is probably *What Little Hans doesn't Learn, Hans won't Learn either* (Was Hänschen nicht lernt, lernt Hans nimmer mehr) (cf. all Herzog 1868).

During the 1970s, this was not seen as currently appropriate. Ivan Illichs demand for a *deschooling* of society saw little use in learning for the future and took it as a waste of time and financial resources. Instead, the required knowledge should be learned when actually needed. This kind of more or less strong reservation can be answered by reassuring ourselves about the origin and the prerequisites of the transition from little Hans to Hans.

The above saying has been traced back to Martin Luther who used it during conversations at the meals: "Was Hänsel nicht lernet, das lernet Hans auch nicht. Die Occasio grüsset dich ... als sollte sie sagen: sieh, da hast du mich, ergreife mich" (What little Hans doesn't learn, Hans won't learn either. The occasion greets you ... as if it was saying: here I am, make use of me). Already during Roman antiquity, the Latin saying "Nam quod in iuventute non discitur, in matura aetate nescitur" existed. Education should start early and unite rigidity and benevolence so as to guarantee educational success.

When taking learning as requiring preconditions, as we sensibly should do in my opinion, then learning cannot be started all of a sudden, but the transition from ignorance to knowledge requires the managing of a number of small transitions. Learning a language, the writing system, calculating – this is exactly why Protestantism for the first time ever established schools on a large scale, so that reading (especially of the Bible) would become possible in the mother tongue.

## Educational theory and transitions

The attempt of approaching the term transition by looking it up in educational dictionaries is hardly successful. It does not exist as a separate entry, neither in French nor English or German publications known to me. It is also a futile attempt to search for the term in the "Enzyklopädisches Handbuch der Pädagogik" edited by Wilhelm Rein. *Übergang* (transition) cannot be found between the entries *Überbürdung* (that is too high demands on the pupils), and *überklug* (that is being precocious which cannot be cured by instruction but only by harm. Also the latest extensive German-speaking encyclopaedia does not have a separate entry but instead refers to *Übergangsquoten* (transitional quota), Übergangsverfahren (transitional processes) and *Übergangszeugnissen* (school reports issued for the transition from primary to secondary schools) in a few places. Only one entry deals with the transition from kindergarten to primary school. The entry hints at problems of cooperation which might help avoiding trouble areas when dealt with.

Also the current and classic specialist literature in educational theory hardly deals with transitions even though it is strong in moral discourse. Only *Friedrich Schleiermacher* refers to the topic in various places in his "Vorlesungen zur Pädagogik" (Lectures on Educational Theory). He introduces for instance the second special part of his "Vorlesungen 1862" (Lectures 1862) by saying that he had discovered two endpoints, that is a maximum and a minimum with regard to the educational influence of family and public life. When contrasting family and public life, a transition emerges which is not exactly definable but a gradual transition without distinct sections ("ein allmählicher Übergang ohne bestimmten Abschnitt", ibid., p 165). Therefore, it is necessary for education to make sections ("Abschnitte zu machen") since the independence of a pupil is nonexistent in the beginning, but complete in the end. But it also seems necessary to him to say that these sections are not distinct but gradual transitions. Schleiermacher thereby marks a certain embarrassment to define transitions in a more narrow sense and to justify an according structure which he regards as necessary. It is particularly this uncertainty and the impossibility to clearly mark it into sections which makes him use the term. This is also notable in other passages. Schleiermacher decidedly demands that society and church should influence an education at a certain point. At a later stage in the education, its subject and the educators would have to come to an agreement as to the choice of profession (ibid., p. 166).

The term transition is introduced also in a few other passages, usually when the author wants to highlight the turn from one state to another. Envisaging the aim of independence would have to be the task of a third period, as he calls it. This period closes the educational development and all those factors meaning personal authority will gradually recede. Meanwhile, it is important to remember that an education can only be completed by a gradual transition (ibid., 179 f.).

On the first glance, *Jean Jacques Rousseau's* work "Emile or on Education" seems to promote by far clearer ideas on transitions. This is already perceivable in his division of the work into five books according to age periods. The period with the greatest risk is, according to Rousseau, the time from birth up to the twelfth year during which no teaching in virtues and wisdom should be carried out. This is substantiated by referring to a "negative education". He says that an education during this time span would not only be useless but even harmful since it would bring to light merely prejudices and bad habits. Instead, it should be aimed for leading a healthy and strong pupil to their twelfth year and to protect their heart from vices and their minds from mistakes.

"If it was only one step from a mother's breast to a reasoned age, today's education would be the right one. But the natural development requires the contrary" (ibid., p. 72). When behaving according to Rousseau's maxims of education and doing the contrary from what was the norm, "the wisest person would be moulded by your hands". "You start by doing nothing and end with an educational miracle" (ibid., p. 73).

The presentation of Emil's education has influenced many educational theorists and developmental psychologists. This is even though it soon becomes clear that the classification of age related phases, such as the 12 years mentioned above, appears rather arbitrary. The uncertainty of Schleiermacher's problem of transition and the theoretical uncertainty are delegated merely to nature and the development itself by Rousseau. On the one hand, he attempts to define a course of events, to mark transitions by dealing with developmental phase-theories. On the other hand, he attempts to distinguish also the didactic, methodological and social potential for an intervention by educators and teachers.

Also *Lawrence Kohlberg*, for instance, deals with the different phases of life – child, youth, adolescent, grown-up, elderly – up to his last and posthumously published book "The Psychology of the Life Span" ("Die Psychologie der Lebensspanne"), clearly following Rousseauian Piaget. He defines the different phases of life as reflexive creations of the senses which follow a course of development organized into phases. According to him, these phases are irritatingly parallel to the cognitive, social (that is the adoption of perspectives) and moral development. Unlike in other developmental psychological approaches, the risks of transition are not so much dealt with as the opportunities arising from contradictions and conflicts. This is precisely what marks transitions as transitions, it is only this which creates the necessary prerequisites for the transition onto the next-higher level (ibid., p. 165 ff). But in distinction to Rousseau and Piaget, the transitions with the clear age-related regulations are softened.

Nevertheless, in a quasi-heroic act, he attempts to attach them to a concept of development which, as many of the newer developmental psychological concepts do, leads far into the age of adulthood and cannot be completed and therefore does not have an age restriction. Development is thereby not anymore perceived as maturing but as a rather metaphoric sequence of constants and transformations in a new temporal-geographical environment. Transitions are then not anymore determined and interpreted on the basis of the biological age but through the course of an assimilating action. A great number of everyday experiences and of scientific studies have shown the restrictions of Piaget's genial experiments. For instance the philosopher Gareth Matthews (1994) reports that his four-year old daughter asked him about infinity when she asked where her cat's flea came from. She was therefore far away from being restricted to pre-conceptual thinking which contradicts Piaget's phases. (Aebli is a lot more careful on the questions of development and phases than Piaget.) Despite obvious short-comings and scepticism about phase-theories and their transitions, the developmental psychological axiom of educational intervention and reflection has been hardly challenged until now in terms of curricula and school lessons. I will be doing this in the rest of this paper by asking for a new standard in education. Transitions are then not primarily related to assumed developmental stages or phases of children and adolescents. Transitions are rather determined by the perspective of social and societal welcoming of aims in education than considered to be made formable by education.

## Transitions as an educational task of forming

This section will unfold a perspective on transition which is probably generally acknowledged, that is the independent, liberty-affirming and self-reflexive human being. For instance Kantian approaches mention the sensible association between guidance from the outside and heteronomy as a prerequisite on the way toward an individual self-development. This leads to a compulsory ethics for educators.

Every human starts life without will, without having wanted to and having approved of it. This action of force by the parents – which starts the transition to individual life – results in their duty to reconcile the child and later the adult with their existence. "In order to manage this settlement of damages successfully, the term 'education' has become established" (ibid., p. 61). The aim of education is, according to Manfred Sommer, the identity of the self which relies on a break-proof and internally sound and continuous intentionality. Education is only considered to have been successful when the individual gives their late consent to their life in liberty which takes much time and patience. This kind of parental or educational attempt is describable by transitions:

> "Those who are being educated go through a sequence of states. The little one becomes older, successively learns more and more things: just sitting, just walking, just speaking [...] All these abilities determine their state in successive order" (ibid., p. 27).

And this kind of state originates in a transition: it links the state of not yet being able to do something with that of now knowing how to do it. Transitions have been successful when the just learned can be applied skilfully, securely and routinely, that is when a new state has been consolidated and settled. Following this stage of *habitualisation*, a new transition may be the next focus. The following demonstrates the structure of the process: a series of states is linked by transitions; the transition unites continuity and innovation (ibid., p. 28). Education therefore guarantees the habitualisation and securing of newly-acquired knowledge. The aim of the educated person is to live without a protective framework provided by others, only such a life is an independent life. Here, (moral) education enters the game when it teaches those who are capable of selfpreservation also to affirm what they know. Education thereby gives intentionality a constitution – in Kantian terms a character which affirms contingency.

## Transitions in the light of educational goals: a (neo-)Aristotelian perspective

Transitions as predominantly generated by education also characterize the following Aristotelian frame. Departing from an understanding of upbringing and education as social (welfare) projects, I will be unfolding and strengthening an approach to transitions which relies on an Aristotelian perspective of a good life. This is with regards to independent and sensible human. The question of how we become independent, practically thinking subjects concerns *Alasdair MacIntyre* in his latest publication "Dependent Rational Animals".

Virtues are defined as praiseworthy conducts which result from respective demands on the social life, and which are graspable ethically and rationally. This understanding goes beyond the frame of ethics of duty and remains entirely within the Aristotelian sense. As Aristotle writes in his second book on Nikomachean Ethics, the rational part of virtue grows from education, the ethical part develops from habit.

MacIntyre now asks how we acquire these virtues and answers the question by assuming a successful education as central element. A faulty education leads us to not recognizing our potential or to only have a narrow consciousness of this potential. Or, on the contrary, to develop no sense for ends to our options and to not realize the difference between realistic expectations and wishful thinking (ibid., p. 91). We hereby require the help and care from parents, teachers etc. and of all that which we generally call education. MacIntyre says that this is why successfully becoming an independent, practically thinking subject is an achievement "even though one which others have contributed to" (ibid., p. 96).

The child needs to learn to distance itself from its own wishes and, for instance, to obey to a mother: "Don't eat that! I know you like it, but it is bad for you" or "this is going to hurt you now, but if! don't do it now, you won't feel better." Children learn the differentiation between their own wishes and decisions on what is good or best for them and others from others. "Both, the good in general and the good for me, has to be learned from others when we aim at being able to decide well for ourselves [...]" (ibid., p. 85).

MacIntyre defines the ability of distancing oneself from immediate wishes, the self-distancing within a social whole and the possibility of unfolding different visions of the future as educational tasks demanding a lot from both the subject and parents and teachers. This distancing is designed to accomplish the transition away from the dependence of childhood to the independence of a rational thinking subject. This requires the possession of speech and the ability to differentiated expression of thoughts.

"The history of every individual going through transitions" is therefore not only an individual history but one of others, their presence, absence and involvement. These others provide the necessary means for the accomplishing of the transition and the necessary social relational frame which allows to gain this independence.

MacIntyre regards education to be a central achievement of society and of its demands which result from those virtues which are not predetermined by nature but also do not go against the nature of man as Aristotle writes in his Nikomachean Ethics. These virtues may be and should be acquired and rely on decisions which allow every individual to deal with others in an independent way and to discuss issues.

In the life of man as well in that of animals of higher orders, patterns of giving and receiving can be observed which go beyond the life span of an individual (ibid., p. 96 ff.). In order to get beyond our natural animal abilities, we require the love and care of others such as mothers, grandparents etc. Without these relationships, we would not be able to develop three main abilities: Firstly, the ability to judge our practical decisions, that is asking whether those reasons for our actions which we believe to be good really are good. Secondly, the ability to realistically envision different developments in the future so that we can rationally select between them. Thirdly, the ability to give up what we wish for in order to obtain a good. Being able to nevertheless free oneself from this integration at a given time, to be independent from what adults want, is another demand which usually causes conflicts. On the other hand, it also demands the ability to let this development not be harmful either for oneself or for others. According to MacIntyre, independence therefore depends on a recognition of dependence. He then summarizes the way toward independence by transitions that need to be mastered.

> "Which characteristics does a child have to develop in order to (...) steer its wishes into a new direction and to (...) consistently aim them at the different phases of its

> life's goods? It has to develop intellectual and moral virtues. Since failing to acquiring these virtues renders it impossible to master this transition, their status and function in human life are immense." (ibid., p. 103)

This does not simply demand an orientation toward what is perceived as comfortable and useful, but, among other factors, an element of restraint which again seems Aristotelian. Neither excesses nor Puritanism, or, referring back to Aristotle, too much physical training is as harmful for the body as too little. Those who shun away from everything become cowardly, those who are not afraid of anything become daring.

Moderation as a virtue will be perceived as comfortable and recognized as useful during the stage of habitualisation, says MacIntyre.

> "The development of the child toward a state in which it is able to step back from its wishes and to judge them is therefore mainly an introduction into those habits which constitute virtues. The child's teachers will have to possess these virtues themselves to a certain degree in order to teach the child." (ibid., p. 104)

Another transition is the fact that there are differences between family and school. A child is firstly treated independent from its performance and virtues by its parents. The obligation of good parents to care well for their child and to convey security and acceptance is given particularly with children who are ugly, ill or retarded. In any case, a child needs to be guided up to the point where it becomes educable also by others such as teachers. In order to reach this stage, it has to be able to distance itself from its own wishes. In this stage, it can judge reasons, revise and exchange them, it develops a feeling for why it acts one way instead of another and also for different situations (ibid., p. 108).

The virtues themselves derive from those practical contexts in which we learn from others – initially from family members, then as a pupil and later as a (farm-) help, worker, teacher, member of a fishing team or of a string quartet. "This is the case since being taught in virtues and the corresponding roles does not mean anything different from learning how to cope with these roles well instead of badly" (ibid., p. 105).

Intellectual and ethical virtues are therefore indispensable in at least two ways, according to MacIntyre: without them, we would be unable to acquire and to continually practice the art of practical thinking, and we would also be unable to care for others appropriately, to educate them so that they also develop the ability of practical thinking. These virtues also protect us from neglect, stupidity etc. Virtues are therefore dominant in their social function – and this is where MacIntyre warns of a too narrow view such as rational choice or homo oeconomicus (ibid., p. 137).

Norms of giving and taking characterize basic social relationships much more profoundly than it is possible to relate in theoretical shortenings or romanticizing variants. Virtues, which we today might also call social competence, demand ways of acting from us which are at the same time just, generous and beneficial. It is this kind of disposition which characterizes educators and should also mark non-calculating giving and just taking. Just generosity is a virtue which is not based on strict proportionality of giving and taking; MacIntyre recommends this attitude also with regard of respect for others. Obviously these virtues initially develop within a close social environment. Nevertheless, this does not stop MacIntyre from transferring the virtue of just generosity also beyond a local community to social intercourse in general. This is because this virtue is embedded in the virtue of an accepted dependence (ibid., p. 194).

According to MacIntyre, the transition from childhood to an independently thinking adult is therefore linked with the acquisition of virtues which not only enable the adult to raise children or a following generation, but also constitute the virtues of behaviour and rationality themselves. Independent thinking is then linked with the virtues of moderation and of just generosity. These are virtues which have become part of ourselves and which we relate to others. We are anything but self-sufficient creatures and thinkers, but we take part in a great number of interactions. Our thinking is therefore also greatly influenced by the action of others.

## Educational institutions and transitions

Speaking Aristotle-like, also institutions introduce into good conduct or should create the prerequisites for society and politics being formable by reason. They should also enable every individual to take action. Performing well in the job and taking part in democratic and political intercourse, requires a great amount of preliminary work in education. This includes especially the virtue of "*just generosity and common discussion*".

According to MacIntyre, this involves moving within a great number of networks of giving and taking and within a great number of social variables which are kept alive (ibid., p. 168f). It is precisely the task of education to ensure that children neither lose themselves within egoism or altruism as the counterpart to the first, that they behave neither self-sacrificingly nor selfishly, but that they find their (social) way of just generosity (ibid., p. 190). To fix this attitude, to change it into a tendency or to transform it, is opposed to attitudes such as narrow-mindedness, self-satisfaction and prejudices against foreigners (ibid., p. 168). It also cannot be restricted by, as I want to add, the world of work which leads to an "erosion of the character" by placing the flexible human entirely within the requirements of the world of work.

To treat citizens in all these areas as free and equal makes it necessary to place them all in the position of at least minimally being able to chose a good way of leading their lives, according to Aristotle. Apart from appropriate working conditions and a health sector, also the educational sector is of central importance for the development of these abilities. This does not primarily mean the distribution of material resources but rather the encouragement of a good way of life through education and professional training, as *Martha Nussbaum* (1999, p. 63 f.) states. When accepting the entire educational sector as, at least, not hindering the spread of reason in society and economy, we can also view transitions within the educational sector and from school to the economy and vice versa from this perspective.

Since the 1990s, a tendency which can be described as a turn away from "universal principles" of education and educational degrees and towards a re-particularization (Zymek 2000) has been observable.

Transitions themselves are newly positioned as part of "the permanent struggle for a stylization and de-stylization of educational offers" (Zymek). This is for instance the case with regards to a new positioning of the employment-area, such as the BA/MA at a university level which also requires new forms of quality management. Also the modulisation of vocational training and further education points in the direction of traditional transitions being in flux. This is exactly why it is important to give access to particulars and divergent attitudes on problems which go beyond the organisation to standards (of welfare) which need to be defined by society and not merely by the interests of single people or bureaucratic requirements.

## Some conclusions

As a first step, we have been concerned with the multi-facetted phenomenon of transitions. Transitions bridge a prior and an after, that is they lead from a status I to a more highly valued status II as regards education (Behrens/Voges 1996). Determination and temporality of education need to self-confidently deal with the paradox of the simultaneity of the un-simultaneous or the necessity of having to infer news from what has already been known. This is the case since a professed aim of these transitions of status is that it will be completed successfully. In order to make such a difference in education and through education formable, a great number of actors is required who build up on previous successes. We have tried to demonstrate this by the example of the dependent independent thinker. We have thereby sketched three main perspectives on transitions.

I would call the first perspective – referring to Schleiermacher – *a sudden change*. Two states are linked (without necessarily tying it to a strong assumption of causality). This transition as a sudden change is noticed by an observer, and it may be wondered what action in terms of education need to be taken to successfully complete this sudden change. According to this model, a transition resembles a black box; this is even though education demands decided foci, that is decisions.

The second perspective will be called *generic*. In this sense, transitions are aimed at a telos the seed of which had already existed. The transition is explainable by the logic of development itself. In the original Rousseauian sense, it is predestined by nature, the newer variants rather explain it through cooperation or interaction between developing individuals and their environment. Education would then be mainly a reaction to a developmental fact which needs to be rendered compatible with the demands of society.

The third perspective is a transition originating from a design-task for *approved social and professional intercourse*. What do we gain by such a developed Aristotelian perspective on education and our topic of transition? To put it briefly: to apply a standard, to strike the right balance and to recognize the nature of education as dealing with preconditions. It helps us to better recognize the basic lines of social goals delegated to the educational system: that is to guarantee the liberty of choice and practical reason (Nussbaum 1999, p. 45). We can now classify the EU's call for lifelong learning in terms of active citizenship and employability, which is uttered in the memorandum I mentioned at the beginning, as their main goal. These two issues require lifelong learning so that we now comprehend them as projects aimed at welfare. It is nevertheless not based on the distribution of goods as Rawls' theory on justice implies (2003), but education should help developing those virtues which create space for the capabilities (Sen 1999) of every individual.

We also refrain from perceiving education merely from the perspective of development. This is except of when we define development broadly – as for instance Hans Aebli does – as the sum of learning processes (ibid., vol. II, p. 352). It also spares us from too thoughtless instant-definitions of learning which can be activated nearly ad hoc and on demand. Education is a social project on which Aristotle applied the standard of good life: "To help one's children and friends to virtue", so that they can then live by a decent occupation and do not evil, neither willingly nor unwillingly. According to Aristotle, this requires good care and education as long as people are young. Later, it requires the law, since also adults should keep these habits (Aristotle, p. 299 f.). The project of a social education will only be successful when "people are capable of issuing laws" (p. 301). Little Hans has to cope with the series of transitions in order to later become a member of society and to help design it. Is this saying old-fashioned? When recapitulating the previous observations, it certainly is not.

Education proves to be a business with many preconditions. This concerns the accumulation of knowledge in itself, but also the temporal dimension. Knowledge and also the virtues of learning have to be learned in a certain order. Only in this way, they can function as a basis for other and new knowledge. But also the point in time of the acquisition of knowledge is important. At a later point, one does not have any time to do so or one is concerned with other, more important issues; for instance, a craftsman has to solve problems concerning his craft.

The business of education also has to deal with preconditions concerning its social component: it needs the involvement of parents, relatives and teachers. (It takes a village to raise a child.) Today, the network of giving and taking is less clear. These transitions are nevertheless and particularly in this case important since independence without predestined paths is tied to an increased dependence; independence is dependent on the cooperation of several actors. The apparent paradox of transition, where the taking part in tradition and continuity clashes with the element of innovation, is thereby solved. Transitions are not only tied with dependences, they also require the striking of the right balance, the balance between a too-much and a too-little.

I vote for perceiving education from the perspective of transition. In case somebody has been thinking about editing a new dictionary on educational theory, I would strongly advise them to not exclude such an entry. On coming back to the Rein-dictionary which I vainly consulted and also quoted at the beginning: Also a too-much in classes and in prudence of adolescents has to do with the Aristotelian balance. In most cases, transitions themselves are a question of balance, that of the teacher and of educational policy in general. A too-much in general demands and particular requirements prove to be as little helpful for the business of education as a permanent too-little in demands. The jungle of certificates, partial autonomies and modular fragmentations render the concern with just generosity and national participation in social life difficult.

## *References*

Aebli, H. : Denken das Ordnen des Tuns. 2 Bd. Stuttgart: Klett-Cotta 1980-81.

Aristoteles: Die Nikomachische Ethik. (translated by O. Gigon) Zurich: Artemis 1951.

Behrens, J./Voges, W.: Kritische Übergange. Statuspassagen und sozialpolitische Institutionalisierung. In: Behrens, J./Voges, W. (Hrsg.): Kritische Übergange. Statuspassagen und sozialpolitische Institutionalisierung. Frankfurt a.M. [u.a.]: Campus 1996, S. 16-42.

European Union: Memorandum for Lifelong Learning. Luxembourg 2000.

Herzog, H.: Das Sprichwort in der Volksschule. Basel: Bahnmaier, 1868.

Kohlberg, L.: Die Psychologie der Lebensspanne. Frankfurt: suhrkamp 2000.

Luther, M./Mulert, H.: Luther lebt! : seine Tischgesprache / ausgew. für unsere Zeit von Hermann Mulert. Berlin: Propyläen-Verlag 1935.

MacIntyre, A.: Die Anerkennung der Abhängigkeit – Über menschliche ) Tugenden. (Amerikan. Original: Dependent Rational Animals. Chicago: Open Court 1999). Berlin: Rotbuch 2001.

Matthews, G.: Die Philosophie der Kindheit. Wenn Kinder weiter denken als Erwachsenene. Weinheim: Quadriga 1994.

Metzler, F. G.: Die Erziehungsweisheit im Sprichwort. Bregenz: Russ 1953.

Muslin, D.: Vor hundert Jahren: Wie Münsterpfarrer Müslin über den Übergang predigte. Bern [s. n.] 1898.

Nussbaum, M.: Gerechtigkeit oder das gute Leben. Frankfurt a. M.: Suhrkamp 1999.

OECD: From Initial Education to Working Life – Making transitions work. Paris 2001.

Rawls, J.: Gerechtigkeit als Fairness. Ein Neuentwurf. Frankfurt a. M.: Suhrkamp 2003.

Rein, W. (Hrsg.): Encyklopädisches Handbuch der Pädagogik. 7 Bände. Langensalza 1895ff. (2. Auflage: 11 Bände. Langensalza 1903ff.)

Rousseau, J-J..: Emile oder Über die Erziehung. Paderborn: Schöningh 1981.

Schleiermacher, F.: Vorlesungen zur Pädagogik. In: M. Winkler/J. Brachmann (ed.): Texte zur Pädagogik. Kommentierte Studienausgabe. 2 Bande. Frankfurt a. M.: Suhrkamp 2000.

Sen, A.: Development as Freedom. New York: A. Knopf 1999.

Siegert, G.: Überklug. In: Rein, W. (Hrsg.): Enzyklopadischen Handbuch der Pädagogik. IX. Langensalza: Beyer 1909, S. 351-352.

Sommer, M.: Identität im Übergang: Kant. Frankfurt a. M.: Suhrkamp 1988.

Tümpel, R.: Überbürdung. In: Rein, W. (Hrsg.): Enzyklopädischen Handbuch der Pädagogik. IX. Langensalza: Beyer 1909, S. 311-325.

Zymek, B.: Re-Partikularisierung des Bildungssystems? Historische Anmerkungen zu aktuellen Strategien der Schulreform. In: Schlömerkemper, J. (Hrsg.): Differenzen. Über die politische und pädagogische Bedeutung von Ungleichheiten im Bildungswesen. Weinheim: Juventa 2000, S. 6-20.

# Politics and education: The discourse of "demographic change"[1]

*Katrin Kraus*

The relationship between politics and education is one of the major concerns in Anja Heikkinen's academic work (e.g. Heikkinen/Kraus 2009). With reference to the discourse of demographic change, this chapter also asks about the effects of policy on the development of education as both science and social practice. The analysis shows that the policies of an aging society are mirrored in education as a process of disciplinary differentiation.

In the following, the relationship between policy and education is analysed using the example of the discourse of demographic change which has recently gained prominence in the industrialised societies and in the European Union (EU). First, I introduce the political discourse about demographic change and its impact on education, including the emergence of the new target group "older employees".[2] Then I discuss the adaptation of education in response to the social change and policy agendas, with emphasis on EU policy in the period of the Lisbon Strategy (2000-10). This is not to deny the importance of recent changes in the age structure of our societies, but it is necessary to contextualise the discussion about those changes and the consequences for education. Finally, the conclusion discusses the findings about these contexts from the perspective of creating target groups in education.

## Demographic change as political discourse and pedagogical issue

In most industrial societies, questions about demographic developments have grown in importance since the beginning of the century. Topics related to the discourse of demographic change include the future of the welfare state, low fer-

1 This contribution began as a paper I presented at the Second Nordic Conference on Adult Education at Linköping in 2007 which I attended with Anja Heikkinen.

2 In the following I talk only about “older employees”. To be more accurate, I should differentiate between older people without employment as “potential older employees” (the aim being to bring them into employment) and “older employees”, who are already employed and the aim is to keep them in employment. Political, pedagogical and human resources strategies are all different, but for the purposes of this chapter, the differentiation is not very important and for reasons of simplicity, it seems appropriate to subsume both as “older employees” even if a part of this group is not employed.

tility rates, the phenomenon of a "greying society", the growing need for care and especially geriatric care, and an impending labour shortage. A much discussed topic in this context has been the duration of working life, welfare costs and labour shortages. Prolonging the average working life has become a political aim. European states have tried to reduce the incentives (and possibilities) for early retirement and to increase incentives for enterprises to keep or take on older employees. Support for older employees to enable (and attract) them to work longer has become a pedagogical issue, especially for vocational and continuing education.

As an example the fifth National Report on Older People by the German Ministry for Family, Senior Citizens, Women and Youth in 2005 (BMFSFJ 2005)[3] gives a brief description of the demographic changes in one European country.[4] This report was done by a group of experts and it presents, in more than 500 pages, the situation of the older generation in various aspects of life, including employment, income, education, family, voluntary work and migration. Among much other data, it shows the increase of the "aged quotient" (*Altenquotient*) and gives a prognosis of its further development. Giving the number of people aged 65+ in relation to 100 people aged between 20 and 64 years, this quotient describes the quantity of old people in a society. For Germany the aged quotient increased from 17.5 in 1953 to 29.3 in 2003, and is estimated to be 54.5 in 2050. These figures may illustrate how the demographic change affects the basic structure of the society. Not only did the figure rise from 17.5 to 29.3 in 50 years, but the rapid and growing pace of the change is also remarkable: The predicted increase for the next 50 years might reach double the speed of the increase in the previous 50 years. Against this background, the report formulates two new targets for education: general adult education should create specific offers for people after retirement and "older employees" should be a special target group for continuing vocational education and in-company training (ibid: 97-125).

The changing structure of age is a significant development, which societies like Germany must recognise. Nevertheless, the recent discourse about this change is too focused on the demographic development itself. Processes of social change and political agendas are important for contextualising this discourse

3 The first German national report on older people was published in 1993; the sixth was published in 2010 with focus on the images of ageing that exists in the German society (BMFSFJ 2010).

4 There are important differences in this discourse between the European countries and it would be instructive to analyse them. For this paper, the important point is the existence of such a discourse in most industrialised countries. I cannot go into detail about how it is processed in different contexts.

and its meaning for education. The question why "older employees" have emerged as a new and important target group for education cannot only be answered with the fact that the future society will consist of fewer younger people and more old ones.

## The transformation of industrial societies

The transformation from industrial to post-industrial economies has had considerable influence on the emergence of older employees as a new target group. This transformation means not only changes to the economy itself but also in the wider society. What sociologists like Giddens and Beck called "individualisation" is one aspect of this transformation in which strict and clear structures and collective institutions are weakened in their function of directing people's lives and guiding individual decisions. The effects for the individuals are two-sided: On the one hand, the scope for personal decisions and self-realisation increases, and on the other hand, so do the economic and social risks.

In industrial society, the lifecycle was pre-structured, with three main phases: childhood and youth as a time for learning and preparation for adulthood; adulthood as a span of employment (for men) and caring for the family (for women), and retirement as the phase of individual aging. This structure served not only as a model for individual life courses but also as a framework for collective institutions, including the field of education, where different sub-disciplines addressed individuals in the three phases of life: young people with schooling and initial vocational education; people active in the labour force with continuing vocational education or in-company training, and the aged population with measures of social work and care.

The relationship between the pre-structured lifecycle of industrial societies and the pedagogical interventions and sub-disciplines of education is illustrated in the following graph showing the model of a (male) employee and the traditional sub-disciplines of education for this lifecycle.

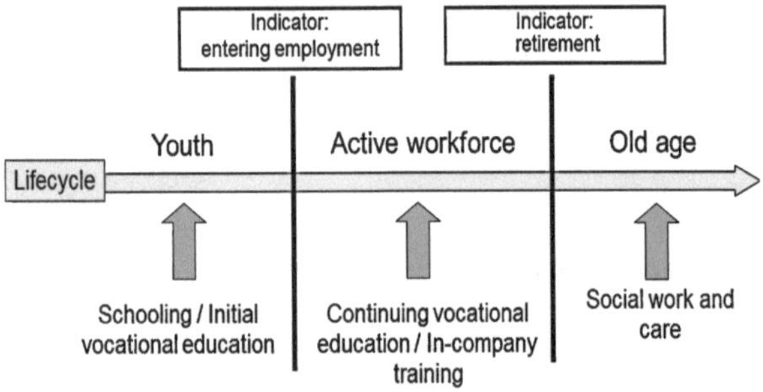


*Graph 1: Lifecycle and education in the industrial model*

In this scheme the main emphasis on learning came in the first third of the lifecycle. Education was seen to be of the greatest importance in the period of youth, not very important during adulthood, and more or less unimportant for the elderly. This scheme was very strict in the German context with its heavy stress on initial vocational training in the Dual System, but was also applied in other European societies.

In the 1970s several international organisations tried to lessen this emphasis on youth learning by promoting permanent education. But only in the late 1990s was the idea established broadly as “lifelong learning”, again promoted by organisations like the EU, the OECD and UNESCO. The revaluation and increasing appreciation of learning as part of the whole lifecycle found broad acceptance in a period when other social structures were changing, too. Since then, the political programme of lifelong learning has found its way into the politics and social norms of European societies. Consequently, the low participation rate of "older employees" in continuing education and in-company training is seen as problematic.

The emergence of “older employees” as a new target group for education results not only from the primarily quantitative phenomenon of more old people and fewer young people, but is also an effect of the aforementioned process of individualisation and de-standardisation of working life and lifecycle in the process of transformation from an industrial to a post-industrial economy. In this process, the formerly relatively clearly distinguished target groups for different forms of education become blurred and the close relations between biological age, employment and education become looser and more flexible. The clear indicator of the transition from “active labour force” to “retirement” has lost its signal function, for instance, because of early retirement, long-term unemployment or voluntary work.

Between the two stages of "active workforce" and "old age", new target groups have emerged that are addressed by specialised education. The following graph illustrates this process of differentiation in education: Older employees are targeted for specialised continuing education or in-company training, whereas for the group of "active oldies", general adult education creates specialised offers. On the one hand, the target group for continuing vocational education and in-company training is divided into those who are addressed by the general programme and the older ones for whom specialised approaches are created. On the other hand, the "active oldies" have become a new target group for general adult education. Third, the target group for social work and care has been shifted to a later stage in the lifecycle.

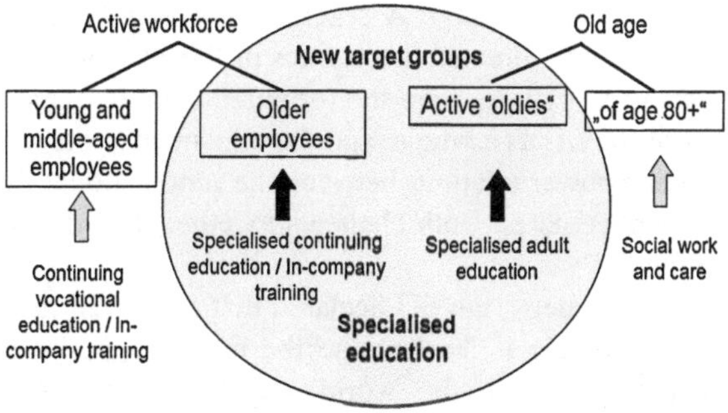


*Graph 2: Differentiation in education*

In this transformation process, education is also forced to redefine and reposition itself. Education's adaptation to the new situation includes the task of addressing new target groups and developing new specialised offers for them. As a consequence, education has undergone a process of differentiation and specialisation. This process is partly a reaction to the demographic change and partly due to the transformation to a post-industrial society in which the strict structures of the industrial societies lost their importance for organising society, its institutions and the lives of the individuals.[5] As mentioned, that has ambiguous consequences for individuals as well as for education: the scope for acting increases but at the same time pressure for a permanent re-orientation emerges.

5 Furthermore, the transformation of welfare states according to neo-liberal principles of less collective and more private responsibility is important here. In this context, one of the targets is to keep people in employment longer in order to reduce public costs for retirement.

Education has lost its clear position in society and meaning in people's lives, but has gained at the same time a new (and larger) role in this process of change. Political forces even give it the task of enabling social change. The role of education is redefined, partly by researchers and practitioners in the field itself, and partly by other actors. In addition, education is expected to moderate the transformation process. This re-orientation of education means that it becomes increasingly differentiated, trying to meet new goals and create new target groups.

## The political context of the EU's Lisbon Strategy

The phenomenon of "older employees" must be seen in its political context - especially of EU policy - since it is this that has changed the framework conditions for education so significantly. A crucial phase is the decade (2000-10) in which the Lisbon Strategy directed the politics of the EU and its member states. The core elements of this strategy are the formulation of an overarching goal for the development of the EU as a whole, and the implementation of a new steering instrument balancing power relations between the supranational EU and the sovereignty of the member states. Both elements together should enable a coherent development of the EU.

With the Lisbon Strategy, the EU declared that an overall goal for its development in the next decade is "to become the most competitive and dynamic knowledge-based economy in the world, capable of sustainable economic growth, with more and better jobs and greater social cohesion" (Presidency Conclusion, paragraph 5). The Lisbon Strategy was re-launched in 2005. In order to prepare the reformulation of its strategy, a "high level group" was installed, chaired by Wim Kok, who reinforced the need for an overarching goal to lead a developmental strategy. "The Lisbon strategy is even more urgent today as the growth gap with North America and Asia has widened, while Europe must meet the combined challenges of low population growth and ageing" (Commission of the European Communities 2005, 4). In the original Lisbon Strategy, globalisation and a knowledge-driven economy were cited as the crucial arguments for a coherent EU strategy (Presidency Conclusion, paragraph 1) and five years later Kok added demographic change as another crucial challenge for Europe's development.

For the "new start" of the Lisbon Strategy, the EU focused on two principle targets: "delivering stronger, lasting growth and creating more and better jobs" (Commission of the European Communities 2005, 7). The details for the second of these targets are important in regards to aging, employment and education. In general they are declared as:

- "Attract more people into employment and modernise social protection systems
- Improve the adaptability of workers and enterprises and the flexibility of labour markets
- Investing more in human capital through better education and skills" (Commission of the European Communities 2005, 9).

The EU makes these targets even more concrete by describing the tasks for member states. The following is one of eight recommendations for achieving the goal of

> "creating more and better jobs: Member States and the social partners must increase efforts to boost the level of employment particularly by pursuing active employment policies which help people in work and provide incentives for them to remain there, developing active ageing policies to discourage people from leaving the workforce too early, and by modernising social protection systems, so that they continue to offer the security needed to help people embrace change" (ibid, 9).

Aging and employment is addressed not only in this paragraph; other paragraphs in the document also refer to demographic change, for instance with focus on the integration of young people into the labour market and increasing migration. The "adaptability of workforce and business" is also one of the requirements, the others being "more and better investment in education and training" and "simplify[ing] the mutual recognition of qualifications" (ibid).

Together with the overarching goal, in its Lisbon Strategy the EU developed the Open Method of Co-ordination (OMC) as a new steering instrument. This instrument is still in operation and involves:

> – "fixing guidelines for the Union combined with specific timetables for achieving the goals which they set, in the short, medium and long term;
>
> – establishing, where appropriate, quantitative and qualitative indicators and benchmarks against best practice in the world and tailored to the needs of different Member States and sectors as a means of comparing best practice;
>
> – translating these European guidelines into national and regional policies by setting specific targets and adopting measures, taking into account national and regional differences;
>
> – periodic monitoring, evaluation and peer review, organised as mutual learning processes." (presidency conclusions, paragraph 37).6

6 The Lisbon Strategy (2000-10) was followed by "Europe 2020. A strategy for smart, sustainable and inclusive growth" (European Commission 2010). With the adoption of the new strategy the EU changed its policies. For the Lisbon Strategy a broad range of structural indicators were used for a periodic benchmarking of member states' perfor-

The OMC comprehends not only timetables, indicators and benchmarks, but also the periodic monitoring, evaluation, and peer reviews of good practice, labelled "mutual learning processes". Part of the procedure is an annual report by member states to the European Commission. Every member state can evaluate its own performance against the EU benchmark as well as in relation to other member states.

Since 1998 the EU has adopted "employment guidelines" that should point all the employment politics of the member states in the same direction. With the Lisbon Strategy, the employment guidelines of the EU have been integrated into the procedure of the OMC. They come with indicators and benchmarks, and thus the responsibilities of member states have increased. With the reformulation of the Lisbon Strategy in 2005, the regularity of the adoption of the guidelines was changed from annual to triennial, as an "integrated package of Employment Guidelines and Broad Economic Policy Guidelines [that] contributes to refocusing the Lisbon Strategy on growth and employment" (EMCO 2005, 1). Eight employment guidelines were adopted by the Council of the European Union in July 2005 for the period 2005-08 (Integrated Guidelines Nos 17 to 24) (Council of the European Union 2005).

The first guideline (No 17) contains the overall aim: "Implement employment policies aiming at achieving full employment, improving quality and productivity at work, and strengthening social and territorial cohesion". As a concrete benchmark for the performance of the member states the Council states: "Policies should contribute to achieving an average employment rate for the European Union (EU) of 70% overall, of at least 60% for women and of 50% for older workers (55–64) by 2010" (ibid, L205/24). Both gender and age are applied as categories to specify the benchmarks for employment. The second guideline is also important for the theme of aging, employment and work: "Promote a lifecycle approach to work". As a more detailed recommendation for the member states, this guideline includes "support for active aging, including appropriate working conditions, improved (occupational) health status and adequate incentives to work and discouragement of early retirement" (ibid; L205/24). A structural indicator here is the "effective average exit age from the labour force", of which the benchmark for 2010 was set at +5 from 59.9 in 2001 (= 64.9).

Besides the conditions of the macro-economic framework, the EU policy sees education and training as crucial for reaching the Lisbon goals, in the original as well as the re-launched version. The EU Commission here takes a human

---

mance. With "Europe 2020", five general targets (so called EU headline targets) are formulated, which must be translated into national targets and strategies.

capital perspective: Investment in education and training of people will result in economic growth and more employment (see for example, Commission of the European Communities 2006). In this context, the focus on the aging population is embedded in the wider strategic goals of the EU for growth and employment, involving sufficient labour force, social cohesion and the restructuring of social security. Being an aspect of the EU employment strategy, it is also directly relevant to the national politics of member states. Education policies are closely interwoven with employment and social policies. All three are part of the overall Lisbon Strategy for the EU, aimed at competitiveness and social cohesion. Education is here seen mainly as instrumental to achieving these goals.[7]

## Conclusion

Constituting older employees as a target group follows the general logic of the creation of target groups in education: first, people are identified by an attribute or a set of attributes as a group, and second, it is argued that the participation of this particular group of people in education is not sufficient – sometimes using a rhetoric of deficit (they need education), sometimes an emancipatory rhetoric (they have the right to education) – and education does not serve their needs, therefore specialised approaches must be developed. In the case of older employees, this results in the following discourse: This target group consists of people aged between 55 and 64 years whose rate of participation in education and the labour market is lower than that of other groups. Since greater participation in education is seen as contributing to a higher employment rate among this age group, increasing their participation in continuing vocational education and in-company training becomes a political task, too. The emergence of “older employees” as a new category is indeed a reaction to demographic developments, but it is also closely related to social change and political agendas.

The influence of political agendas reaches beyond the political area as such, touching the field of research and social practices such as education without direct imposition. It is not only the mechanism of "governing by numbers" or fi-

7 The politics referred to in this chapter are those of the period 2000-05 when the issue of aging gained more and more importance in EU policy. The topic remains important, so the year 2012, for example, has been declared the "European Year of Active Ageing and Solidarity between Generations". Also in the meantime, aging has been the topic of several EU documents, including "The Demographic Future of Europe - from Challenge to Opportunity" (2006), "Promoting Solidarity between the Generations" (2007) and "Dealing with the Impact of an Ageing Population in the EU (2009 Ageing Report)" (2009). In November 2010, the European Parliament adopted a resolution entitled "Demographic challenge and solidarity between generations".

nancial incentives that make political agendas influential. It is also the discursive phenomenon of opening "windows of opportunity" for a specific development in sciences and social practices. Discourses such as the one about "demographic change" create spaces for questions and topics that had not been possible without them. Yet it is not politics alone that creates these opportunities. As argued here, the embeddedness of education (as science and social practice) in the historic context of a distinct society must also be taken into account. The "windows of opportunity" for specific topics arise in the interplay of political agendas of different actors, and the changing social norms and expectations of a society.

## *References*


BMFSFJ (= Bundesministerium für Familie, Senioren, Frauen und Jugend) (2005): Fünfter Bericht zur Lage der älteren Generation in der Bundesrepublik Deutschland. Potenziale des Alters in Wirtschaft und Gesellschaft. Der Beitrag älterer Menschen zum Zusammenhalt der Generationen. Bericht der Sachverständigenkommission. Berlin. August 2005. (availability, last download 02/02/2012: http://www.bmfsfj.de/BMFSFJ/Service/Publikationen/publikationsliste,did=151512.html)

BMFSFJ (= Bundesministerium für Familie, Senioren, Frauen und Jugend) (2010): – A New Culture of Ageing. Images of Ageing in Society - Findings and recommendations of the Sixth German Government Report on the Elderly. Berlin. November 2010. (availability: http://www.bmfsfj.de/BMFSFJ/Service/Publikationen/publikationsliste,did=176124.html last download 02/02/2012)

Commission of the European Communities (2005): Communication to the Spring European Council: Working together for growth and job; A new start for the Lisbon Strategy. Communication from the President Barroso in agreement with Vice-President Verheugen. (COM(2005)24 final). (availability, last download 02/02/2012 http://eur-lex.europa.eu/LexUriServ/LexUriServ.do?uri=COM:2005:0024: FIN:en:PDF)

Commission of the European Communities (2006): Commission Staff Working Document. Progress towards the Lisbon Objectives in Education and Training. Report 2006. (SEC(2006)639). Brussels, 16.5.2006. (availability, last download 02/02/2012: http://ec.europa.eu/education/lifelong-learning-policy/doc/report09/report_en.pdf)

Council of the European Union (2005): Council decision of 12 July 2005 on Guidelines for the employment policies of the Member States (2005/600/EC). Source: Official Journal of the European Union (L205/21; 6/8/2005) (availability, last download 02/02/2012: http://eur-lex.europa.eu/smartapi/cgi/sga_doc? smartapi!celexplus!prod!Doc Number&lg=en&typedoc=Decision&an_doc=2005&nu_doc=600)

EMCO (= Employment Committee) (2005): Indicators to monitor the Employment Guidelines (2005 – 2008), EMCO, October 2005.

European Commission (2010): Europe 2020. A strategy for smart, sustainable and inclusive growth. EN. COM(2010). Brussels, 3.3.2010 (availability: http://eur-lex.europa.eu/ LexUriServ/LexUriServ.do?uri=COM:2010:2020:FIN:EN:PDF; last download 05/01/2007)

European Parliament / Council of the European Union (2011): Decision No 940/2011/EU of the European Parliament and of the Council of the European of 14 September 2011 on the European Year for Active Ageing and Solidarity between Generations (2012). Official Journal of the European Union 23.9.11; 246/5 (availability: http://eur-lex.europa.eu/LexUriServ/LexUriServ.do?uri=CELEX:32011D0940:EN:NOT; last download 01/02/2012)

Heikkinen, Anja / Kraus, Katrin (eds.) (2009): Reworking Vocational Education. Policies, practices and concepts. Peter Lang: Bern et al.

Presidency Conclusions, Lisbon, 23/24 March 2000 (availability: http://www.consilium.europa.eu/uedocs/cms_data/docs/pressdata/en/ec/00100-r1.en0.htm; last download 02/02/2012)

# Reforms in Norwegian VET and hegemonic influences from general education

*Ole Johnny Olsen*

As a contribution to a volume celebrating Anja Heikinnen and her lifelong involvement for research, teaching and intellectual engagement in the field of vocational education and training, I will give a short account on some aspects of the reform processes within Norwegian VET. The theme, I thrust, relates to one of her central interests of knowledge, the condition for autonomy and recognition of the pedagogical field of VET.

## Two roads for equality in Norwegian educational politics

Much of the educational politics as well as the sociology of education in Norway has been oriented towards, or shaped by, the concept of equality, not least since the 1950s and 60s. Two main routes have been followed to reach the goal of equality. One route has been informed by the idea of providing equal opportunities for all in climbing the educational ladder. Here, the main means have been the building of schools, the extension of the years of compulsory school, scholarships, and cheap loans for university education. The second route has been based on the idea of equality through the institutional integration of different school systems and the development of one kind of school for all. At the compulsory level, this route was already established at the end of the 19th century in the model of the 'unity school'. Since World War II, the model has been a central premise in every educational reform. A big advance for the unity school was the establishment of the comprehensive lower secondary school, the 'youth school', in the 1960s, whilst a further step along the way was the integration of the gymnasium and the vocational school into one system of comprehensive upper secondary education in the 1970s.

At the level of upper secondary education, the changes contained in Reform 94 carried forward both of these routes, the first by a 'reform of rights', which gave every 16 year old the right to three years of further education. The second route was extended firstly by a structural reform, the purpose of which was the inclusion of different authorities and channels of resources in a single new educational structure and secondly, by a reform of content. The latter involved the reconstruction of the curriculum both at the general level and within the particular fields of disciplines and vocational trades. Reform 94, as a whole, was seen as completing the educational edifice set up to incorporate and house the two main traditions: the general tradition (the gymnasium) and the specific vocational tradition (building on apprenticeship regulated by the partners of working life).

Since the 1990ies the rights of upper secondary education has been extended to all younger than 24 years of age and the integration of VET into the general upper secondary education has been strengthened as far as both structure and content is concerned.

In the light of a concept of equality as equal worth, a closer look at both the routes outlined above gives reason to question some of the ends which they serve. Firstly, at the centre of political interest, there has always been the matter of 'formal rights' within the vexed question of equal opportunities. Educational rights have been directed towards the supporting of individuals with educational certificates and identities (Halvorsen 1994) and the reasoning underlying that thrust can be summarised as follows: The basic idea has been that education, with its formal merits, is the fundamental asset if you want to get ahead in life. In order to reach the higher goals, you need higher education. By developing the 'educated' citizen, the problem of social inequality should be solved. This has formed the guiding line for all the conservative parties as well as the Norwegian Labour Party. For the latter, this policy has produced a kind of historical irony. Its function (if not also the goal) has been the integration of the working class into the society by giving working class youngsters middle class education and opportunities (ibid).

Secondly, this middle class orientation of educational politics has had an even stronger manifestation in the cultural primacy, or even hegemony, of general education. Given a focus upon formal rights, it also follows that a focus upon formal, general education is naturally subsumed. Further, the tradition of working class training, with its emphasis upon practical knowledge, drawn from experience and working life, together with the standards and norms founded on daily work and co-operation, cannot be said to have formed the ideal of educational progress. In the political climate of the late 1960s, traditional vocational education, regulated by working life through the apprenticeship system, was seen as an anachronism. General academic disciplines and theoretical knowledge were both regarded as more relevant to further education and lifelong learning and as constituting the basic means of enhancing economic growth, enabling mobility in the labour market and fostering the individual careers of tomorrow. The following statement, made in 1969 by the youth organisation of the Labour Party, expresses in a highly significant way the ideology of the time: "Just as it was important to get the Act of Apprenticeship in the 1930s, it is equally important to get rid of it today" (quoted in Halvorsen 1994:106).

The historical scrapping of the apprenticeship institution was based on the goal of developing the unity school system even further. From my point of view, it also underscores two other elements of the political tradition of education in Norway. The first is the question of what is seen as the best place of learning. This question has generally, almost self evidently, been answered with the idea that the school is the natural and best place of learning. This idea contrasts quite strongly with the view, born of experience, that the school is, most of all, a place of socialisation. However, the learning of particular kinds of knowledge often has a much better chance in situations other than those inside classrooms. The second element concerns the concept of knowledge. The dominance of theoretical knowledge has been strong. Theory has been valued as more important and more connected to higher status than has the practical knowledge used in action, whether on the shop floor of industry or by the bed in the hospital. This stands, in fact, in contrast to a growing recognition of the importance of situated learning and of practical knowledge within the field of education and training during the last decades. The question is, however, to what extent – if at all – these insights have been taken as point of departure in developing actual educational policies and institutional reforms.

It turned out that the politicians of the 1960s were wrong in their predictions of the future of vocational education and the apprenticeship system. The apprenticeships system did not die out. On the contrary, it experienced a renaissance in the 1970s and 80s, via a rise in the number of apprentices, a new act and an increase in new occupational trades. Reform 94, in fact, caught this new interest in apprenticeship and set up the goal of developing vocational education, building on the regulative principles of vocation trades. A big challenge for vocational education, however, was how to escape the institutional power and cultural hegemony of general education in the process of integration. It might be suggested that vocational education came under strong pressure from the ideals and standards of general education, and that this pressure today is stronger than it has been for a long time. I will present some indicators supporting this suggestion and discuss some problematic consequences of the pressure both at the institutional level and for the individual students within vocational education. Generally, the discussion deals with the problematics of integration, standardisation and normalisation.

## Institutional, integrational and hegemonic traditions

So far, I have argued that Norwegian educational politics have been dominated by the idea of the utility of general education, the goal of social mobility through educational rights and the idea of the educated citizen as the ultimate individual identity. Altogether, one might say, Norwegian education has built on a cultural hegemony of theoretical and general education and upon a predominant tradition, which sees the classroom as the optimal place of learning. The following elements of political and institutional initiatives and actions may be seen as expressions of, and support for, these hegemonic traditions.

One element is the Education Act of 1999, which integrated all levels and different education and training routes for all, from 6 to 19 years of age, by replacing three separate acts: the act on primary and secondary compulsory school, the act on upper secondary education and the act on apprenticeship and vocational training. The act on apprenticeship and vocational training had played a very important role, both by expressing and supporting the identity of the tradition of vocational training and by securing its regulative autonomy. Now, this distinctive basis for identity and autonomy was removed.

This should not be taken to mean that the apprenticeship system totally disappeared in the new act. In principle, the system still keeps some of its relative autonomy. However, what is set down in writing may be one thing, whilst what happens in daily life can be quite another. Already, the presentation of the new act from the ministry of education showed how the dominant ideas within the same ministry tend to reduce, and even to remove, the distinct existence and autonomous position of vocational training and apprenticeship. A pamphlet that was spread as information of the new act in 1999 presented the new system with the following heading (the italics are mine): "New common educational act: *a comprehensive school system"*. Already here, the two years of apprenticeship within firms had disappeared. Moreover, the text directly following confirmed the impression, viz, "It is now a joint *school cours*e from six years of age, with the right to education on the level of further education." It went on: "The *school system* now gets a new act". On all the six pages containing information on the new law, only one small paragraph was devoted to vocational training. There, the whole tradition was reduced to an educational regulation of training, partly in school and partly in a company. The small paragraph began: "... further education can *also* be taken in the form of vocational training...", thereby emphasising the exceptional character of that "form". Apprenticeship and the system of craft based learning were out of the horizon of the people in ministry of education.

At the administrative level, we have seen much the same tendency. The ministry of education was reorganised. Separate departments for specific levels and educational routes were closed down. One department for all education, from primary to upper secondary, was set up. Within the ministry, the distinctive expertise of distinctive education, for example, vocational education does not form the founding principle. And even more important, the training councils for each trade, consisting of representatives of the trade itself, have been weakened. Traditionally, these councils were key participants within the dynamics of vocational training, representing important vocational training expertise, taking part in discussions of change, involved in political decisions and taking initiatives for innovations. Now, the councils have been reorganized, representing larger fields of different trades and reduced to bodies entitled merely to comment and advice. Regional councils, traditionally holding influential positions for the regulations of local vocational education, have gone through similar changes.

Through different institutional change we can observe a weakening of the autonomy and unique character of the Norwegian vocational education. The danger of that distinctive character and quality disappearing, through the integration of vocational education into a larger whole, seems to have been common in the history of this field. The trend began in vocational education with the old 'work shop schools' many years ago (cf. Kokkersvold/Melde, 1982). It now threatens the rest of vocational education, both at the institutional and cultural levels. On the cultural level, the following instances are telling. Through various processes of integration the field of vocational education is left without a separate, dedicated periodical for information, discussion, academic articles, exchanges of teachers' experiences, book reviews or what ever. This process began with the disappearance of the journal *Yrkesopplæring* (vocational training/education) published by the governmental and corporate council Yrkesopplœringsrådet, from 1933 to 1977. With the integration of vocational training under the common law for all upper secondary education in 1974, this journal was incorporated into the newly established journal entitled *Videregående opplæring (*upper secondary education). Around 1990, the whole system of councils for the ministry of education was reorganised and partly closed down. In 1993, the ministry itself established a journal with a highly professional layout and an ambitious programme, named *Schola - journal for education.* After three years, the publication ceased. Today, the whole public/governmental system of education is left with general information on the homepage of the Educational directorate.

A similar process can be seen with regard to the vocational teachers' organisation. The journal of Norsk Faglærlag (Norwegian vocational teachers' organisation) established in 1947, with the name *Yrke (*occupation), incorporated two former journals as a result of the integration of their respective organisations: the journal for housekeeping teachers in 1973 and the journal for commercial teachers in 1974. In the eighties and early nineties, *Yrke* was a strong voicepiece for the vocational teachers' ambition for further professionalization. To what extent this ambition informed the decision to become part of the new organisation for all teachers at the upper secondary level, is not clear. Whether or not this was the case, the decision was made. From 1993, the vocational teachers became members of Lœrerforbundet (Teachers' Union). The new journal is entitled *Skolefokus* (Focus on the School), hardly associative with the traditional vocational teachers.

## Institutional hegemony and consequences for the students

What then have been the consequences of this institutional integration for vocational education students within the hegemony of general education? Even though more and more young people take the route of general upper secondary education it remains the case that around half the students in each age group still make their choice within vocational education. Why is this so? Very often, sixteen year old boys and girls do not know exactly what they want to do. There might be a special interest in some kind of craft, or in some particular form of work, but this is, in fact, more the exception than the rule. The interests and reasons guiding their educational choice, though various, and often complex in character, are frequently more general than specific. Those who take the vocational route know one thing first and foremost: they do not want to take the road of general education. They are fed up with a school where only theory reigns; they want 'something practical', whether it is dealing with art, cooking, 'technical things', or 'human things'. This picture was one of the strongest and clearest to emerge during our research, carried out as part of the evaluation of Reform 94 (see Olsen/Seljestad, 1996 1997, Arnesen 1997, Bjørnstad 1997, Grov 1998). And the picture held, not only for the 'weaker' students, although their depiction was the strongest, but also for those whose grades were certainly good enough to take the general route. They too wanted a change - something different - something practical. They knew that they could pursue the general disciplines needed for higher education later. If they wanted to do so (and most likely they would (Arnesen 1997), that was for later, but not just now. Various projects have showed similar results since then.

But what do the students meet in their first year at the vocational schools? After Reform 94, much more than previously, they met a situation in which the range of disciplines were not dissimilar from that in general education. They encountered a very broad curriculum with small 'experimental' tastes of different crafts or occupational work, often within a classroom situation. In technical fields, they undertook three days in classrooms and two days in the workshop - if they were lucky. They were confronted with projects very much like the ones they had experienced in lower secondary school, which often demand the skills involved in handling 'theoretical' matters and problems and in writing reports which fit the expectations and discipline of the conventional Norwegian school. One consequence was that much of the motivational power, which can be realised by doing 'real things', were lost at this level. Students were disappointed; those who had most problems with the self-discipline of classroom learning were the greatest losers.

Even in the second year, at the more specialised level of the school component of vocational education, a high degree of classroom teaching was to be found, for example, by those undertaking the course for care workers. Here, they experienced one or two week visits to a work place for practical work and view it as *the* happening of the year (Olsen/Seljestad 1997). That was also true for those students who had more workshop experience. The young electrician and plumber students interviewed by Tomas Bjørnstad in his master's project provided a good example. They found the experience of two weeks in a company extraordinarily instructive: "It's like night and day. You learn much more in the company. We had fourteen days of practical learning there and I certainly learned just as much as I learned in two months at school," concluded an electrician student (Bjørnstad 1977:60). Of course, school study is also necessary, they would maintain: "If you hadn't been at school, you would have been totally green and wouldn't understand anything." (ibid: 59). Their clear opinion was that the real learning, learning real work, was best done within the experience of working life. There, you learn to do things quickly, and seriously:

> You get a pressure on yourself. And if you don't manage something, they say,"Hey, can't you do that?"And then they show you real fast and you have to be very concentrated to see what they are doing. But here, here it's more school-like, right?" (plumber student, ibid.:61)
>
> You are much more motivated when you are out in a company. Then you want to learn, then. It's almost like, like, you have to, in a way. Then you have to keep up, you can't sit and sleep. Like here, you can sit and fool around all day (plumber student, ibid: 62).

These kinds of attitudes and experiences among young people within vocational education and training are also very well documented in earlier research in the field, not least in the extensive apprentice project of Liv Mjelde from the early 1980s (see Mjelde 1987, 1993). Here, we also learned how the students insisted on the necessity of seeing the connection between what they are doing in school and what they need for doing real work. If this connection is severed, the meaning of school work is lost, as is the motivation. On the other hand, it is the experience of making 'real things' and of seeing concrete results which give the learning point and meaning (cf. Edvardsen 1985), along with real joy and the self confidence of being capable. As the young plumber student, quoted in the title of Bjørnstad's master's thesis, observed: "It's quite fun when you experience that you *can* do something."

In a new reform in 2006 some of the vocational programs were made even broader than before, encompassing the preparation for more trades. But some initiatives were also taken to meet part of the criticism against the broad and general curriculum. Both at the first and second year the students will choose special and practical "projects for going in depth". For some these projects are fruitful, for others they are of less relevance. Evaluation research on these reform initiatives is still not completed.

Some students find out during the first two years of vocational school that the route is not for them and they try to switch to general education, or want to do something else. This was observed already in the 1990ies (Arnesen 1997, Bjørnstad 1997). Today the tendency of switching to general education has been much stronger, and seems as one of the most serious challenges for the future of vocational education. Most students, however, still have the opposite orientation. Principally, they are looking forward to life as an apprentice, as observed in the 1990ies (Olsen/Seljestad 1997). The picture is clear: they want to get into 'real life', they want to earn their own money and they want to do real work. Their expectations and their valuations of coming into the 'real life' may sometimes seem to be no more than an idealistic, romantic view of working life. There is, however, a range of values which these young people see in, and expect from, working life, and which needs to be taken seriously. Among them are the importance of doing 'real things', of being responsible for serious work and of being in relationships of interdependence. These are strong elements in the positive expectation of the new real life, and these elements are confirmed by the experience of apprenticeship. After a while in apprenticeship, their experience of the good side of that life is reported with statements of having 'good colleagues' who help and take care of them the best they can. Beside the value of doing and learning interesting work and earning their own money, the most positive and general value the apprentices express is the feeling of social belonging (Olsen/Seljestad 1999, Flaatten 1999).

## Conclusion

There is no doubt of the existence of the distinctive character of Norwegian vocational education and there is no doubt of its considerable value, for the development of capacities and skills in young workers and for good learning experiences and for positive effects on the personal development of those young people taking that educational route. Problems arise, however, when the unique character of this system is put under pressure by a general process integrating the different systems and traditions into one institutional order. In this process, there has been, and continues to be, a tendency, with all the attendant dangers for vocational education, for the stronger general education tradition to dominate. As a consequence, the institutional autonomy of vocational education has, to some extent, been eroded. At the level of the individual, students have lost much of the possibilities of those routes which have been capable of recognising and catering for different motivations, interests and goals.

## *References*


Arnesen, Ellen Cathrine (1997): "Studiekompetanse? Kjekt å ha, kan få bruk for det en vakker dag…" Utdannings- og yrkesorientering hos elever på yrkesfaglig studieretning etter innføring en av Reform 94. AHS Serie A 1997-4, Universitetet i Bergen

Bjørnstad, Tomas (1997): "Det er gøy når du merker at du kan noe." Skoleerfaringer og arbeidslivsorienteringer blant elever på elektrofag og rørfag vk1, AHS Serie A 1997-3, Universitetet i Bergen

Edvardsen, Edmund (1985): Å føye sammen det atskilte. Dissertation. Universitetet i Tromsø

Flaatten, Sandra Val (1999): Bedriften som arena for læring, opplæring og sosialisering. En sosiologisk undersøkelse av fagopplæring ved Hydro Porsgrunn Industripark, AHS Serie A 1999-1, Universitetet i Bergen

Grov, Håvard (1998): "Hjemmekjær eller reiselysten? Elever på yrkesfaglig studieretning i Sunnhordland etter innføringen av Reform 94", AHS Serie A 1998-1, Universitetet i Bergen

Halvorsen, Tor (1994): "Forskning om yrkesutdanning og yrkesliv. Hvor går vi nå?" in Jon Lauglo: Norsk forskning om utdanning. Perspektiver og veivalg. Oslo: Ad Notam Gyldendal

Kokkersvold, Erling & Liv Mjelde (1982): Yrkesskolen som forsvant. Oslo: Gyldendal

Mjelde, Liv (1987): "From hand to mind", in David Livingstone (ed): Critical Pedagogy and Cultural Power. Mass.: Begin & Garvey Publishers.

Mjelde, Liv (1993): Apprenticeship. From Practice to Theory and Back Again. Dissertation. University of Joensuu Publications in social Sciences, No 19

Olsen, Ole Johnny og Lars Ove Seljestad (1996): "Utdanning som utvikling - ambisjoner og erfaringer i yrkesfaglig opplæring" in Blichfeldt J.F. et al.: Utdanning for alle? Oslo: Tano-Aschehoug.

Olsen, Ole Johnny og Lars Ove Seljestad (1997): Læreplaner og framtidsplaner. Evaluering av Reform94. AHS Serie B 1997-2, Universitet i Bergen

Olsen, Ole Johnny og Lars Ove Seljestad (1999): Opplæring i bedrift etter Reform 94 – nye krav og utfordringer for fagopplæringen, in Rune Kvalsund et al. (eds): Videregående opplæring - ved en skillevei? Oslo: Tano Aschehoug

# On comparing. Or: The struggle for history and culture. A tribute to Anja Heikkinen

*Matthias Vonken*

When I was asked to write an essay for an anthology for Anja's anniversary, the demand was not to write a scientific article as usual but something "what I ever wanted to say to Anja". This is quite a challenge for me because usually it isn't a problem to talk to her in a direct way and I thus haven't much to say what I couldn't do in one of the annual conferences. But then I remembered the issue of history and culture and its unsolved problems and innumerous attempts to include them in the work of the "VET & Culture Network"...

The VET & Culture Network, for which Anja is some kind of spiritus rector, wants to bring together researchers and scholars from Europe and (in the meantime) from all over the world to discuss issues e.g., concerning comparative VET with a cultural and historical perspective. That is so far part of the program.

As I joined the network during the conference in Erfurt in 2002, many aspects of very different parts of VET were discussed, besides the role of history and culture. In the following years, this was perpetuated. In every conference there was a part on reflections of the network and its future, and always Anja demanded to include the role of history and culture more than it happened in the past. Nothing changed. In the conference in Arvidsjaur in 2008 we committed to start a proceeding on the role of history and culture in the comparison of VET. I incautiously promised to start this proceeding with an essay on principles of comparing. It might be a little bit late now, but perhaps this essay could serve as the late fulfillment of my promise.

## Preliminary thoughts – on comparison and epistemology

Let us make some preliminary and preparing assumptions: Comparison is a matter of comparing, of course. The leading question is: How can we compare things? One answer was given by Immanuel Kant (Kant, 2003). Everything we know has two possible sources: the mind or the experience. Judgments can be made by thinking or by making and comparing experiences. That is Kant's distinction between the world of experience (which exists only a posteriori) and the world of mind (which is possible a priori). It delivers two kinds of possible judgments: the synthetic and the analytic. Knowledge in the world of experience means to compare one experience with another. If we add the assumption that experiences can only be gained by our senses, and these senses can fail (Maturana & Varela, 1987), then experience is not the way for gaining objective knowledge about something. It will always be contaminated by the possibility of errors of our senses. It leads to a synthetic judgment a posteriori. In this sense, objectivity can only be reached in the world of mind in which we don't compare experiences but make analytic judgments. These are judgments a priori, i.e. before any experience and without the necessity of having experienced the subject of our knowledge. Kant itself used mathematics as an example for analytic judgment a priori. However, this world of mind naturally lacks in experience which is quite difficult if we want to compare something in the real world like VET. We can thus decide not to be objective in comparing or to not compare at all. We will discuss this problem later.

Nevertheless coming back to the topic of comparison in VET, we first have to judge how to compare. Educational systems – and VET of course is some kind of a part of a system, whether it is institutionalized or not – usually are not invented at some point of history but grow during a longer period inside a society. They fulfil different demands of society which change by time and along changes of the society itself. To compare such system parts we should understand the systems first. And to understand a system we thus need to understand the history and the culture of the system and of the particular society in which the system evolved.

Of course other ways are possible. One might say that you don't need to be a tomato to judge about ketchup. In this sense we can compare systems or parts of them without knowing too much about the system's history. We can e.g., conduct a study about dropouts in apprenticeships in Finland, Norway and Sweden, and we will probably find different dropout rates in the different countries. However, to deeply interpret the results we need to know not only details of the systems but why a system is as it is and how it evolved. Then we can judge e.g., if dropout is really a problem in a country and what kind of activities would be necessary to avoid the problem in another country. Let me give another example: One aim of international development aid is to foster VET in less developed countries. In the past we can find attempts to transfer a VET approach from one country to another. Knowing the fact that VET is always the result of the development of a specific country, those attempts are doomed to failure if the receiving country has experienced a different historical and cultural development. It would just not fit the needs of the society. Adjustments are necessary, and these can only be made in view of the knowledge about the history and culture of the country.

## Comparing as a matter of mind

If we accept the assumption of the necessity of knowledge and understanding of history and culture of the VET systems of those countries which we want to compare, we face the next problem: how to get this knowledge, how to understand the development. It seems to be obvious that getting knowledge about the history and culture of a foreign country means to get knowledge by experience in Kant's meaning. We cannot judge about history and culture a priori because both are aspects of the ontic world and need to be 'experienced' to some extent. Therefore, we have to collect data and information and to interpret the results. However, interpreting is a work of mind, and this work has some rules and some preconditions.

The way in which we do this work of mind is bound to our own cultural background which we cannot leave. Every researcher is born in and bound to his or her own culture. That implies the way of thinking and furthermore, the way of researching and interpreting. According to George H. Mead, the development of mind and language is from gesture to symbol to significant symbol (Mead & Morris, 2000) (i.e. experience). This happens inside a given society, i.e. what we identify as a significant symbol depends on our own culture. If for example someone in Bulgaria shakes his/her head it usually means to agree to something while in most other cultures it would be a denial. Even in one country or inside one language community we can face such examples. In the region of Thuringia in Germany the word "no" means "yes". In most other parts of Germany this would be interpreted as the English phrase for denial. In Switzerland it is widely used to end nearly every sentence with "oder?" (in English something like "isn't it?"). To German speaking people from outside Switzerland this means a request to give a statement or an answer. In fact it mostly is only a phrase to end a sentence without requesting anything.

Identifying something as a significant symbol thus is a learning process that takes part in the given society someone lives in. Even if we learn foreign languages and in this context other significant symbols, we usually are not able to catch all the meanings and backgrounds of a significant symbol (a word, a phrase etc.) of a foreign society as long as we don't live in it for an adequate time. And as researchers we usually don't have the opportunity to move to a country for several years, which we want to study. Interpreting data and information for the matter of comparison thus is the attempt to judge about facts in view of our own significant symbols, in view of our own culture and history, which we cannot escape. It is our lifeworld ("Lebenswelt") which gives us our opportunities to judge about facts and data, and which we usually don't scrutinize (see Habermas, 1987, pp. 171ff.). It is one more cause why synthetic judgments a posteriori cannot be objective. It can only give us weak results. For the reasons that came from the thoughts of Mead and others the facts even cannot be fully understood because the researchers are missing the real meanings of the necessary significant symbols.

## To compare or not to compare: that's the rule

This all sounds disappointing. We cannot make analytical judgments a priori (which would be objective) because comparing needs the empirical world. We cannot (easily) understand the empirical world of a different culture because we are bound to our own lifeworld. We should thus give up trying to compare VET in the view of history and culture. Luckily Kant gave us a third way to solve this dilemma.

Getting to know facts, history and culture of a country is undoubtedly a matter of making experiences. How deep this knowledge can be depends on how intensive we experience the experiences. We thus should first try to do comparative work together with colleagues sharing the life-world of the targeted countries. This is quite a simple conclusion and often difficult to realize. The second best way is to study intensively history and culture of targeted countries while keeping always in mind that we judge about something which we only experience in a second order from the standpoint of an observer and bound to our own understanding of certain facts coming from our lifeworld.

The second point is the comparison itself. While we can only compare experiences concerning our topics of VET, the *way* of comparing doesn't necessarily have to be analytical in Kant's sense: "For whence could our experience itself acquire certainty, if all the rules on which it depends were themselves empirical, and consequently fortuitous?" (Kant, 2003, p. 44, translated by J. M. D. Meiklejohn, English citation from Project Gutenberg). If we want to do a proper comparison we thus have to think about the *rules* of comparing. And these rules shouldn't be derived from experiences (and thus preferably not from the lifeworld), but they should result from pure thinking. If we can avoid using experiences for constituting the rules for comparing, we find the second best way to a pure knowledge a priori, an "impure": "For example, the proposition, 'Every change has a cause,' is a proposition a priori, but impure, because change is a conception which can only be derived from experience" (ibid., 43). The same applies to rules for comparing. They can only be derived from the experiences we made in studying facts, history and culture. But they can be a priori in the sense that the rules for comparing the items can be found by "pure reason", i.e. by logic.

## In the end

What I ever wanted to say to Anja is now: Don't struggle with the accommodativeness of the network if we don't consider history and culture in our work. We now have some reasons for this circumstance. And perhaps we can find a way out in starting a discussion about how these rules could be constituted by thinking intensively and without mixing up the thinking too much with own experiences.

*References*

Habermas, J. (1987). Theorie des kommunikativen Handelns. Band 2: Zur Kritik der funktionalistischen Vernunft (4th ed.). Frankfurt a.M.: Suhrkamp.

Kant, I. (2003). Kritik der reinen Vernunft u.a. (Ungekürzte Neuausg. der historisch kritischen GA, Sonderausg.). Wiesbaden: Fourier.

Maturana, H. R., & Varela, F. J. (1987). Der Baum der Erkenntnis. München: Goldmann.

Mead, G. H., & Morris, C. W. (2000). Mind, Self, and Society: From the standpoint of a social behaviorist (29th ed., Vol. 1). Chicago: Univ. of Chicago Press.

# On gender, work, vocationalism and VET

*Liv Mjelde and Manfred Wahle*

## The personal is political (Liv Mjelde)

The question of gender has been an underlying concern in all VET & Culture conferences, but two of the conferences have directly addressed the subject as it pertains to vocational education. The first one took place in Tampere in May 1996 where the theme was the gendered history of vocational education. Its primary aim was to discuss themes and methods for developing gendered historical research on vocational education in a European perspective.[1] What did we know about women's life and work situations in the different European countries at different points in history? What about the ideology of housewifery and women in different eras? The historian Ruth Watts was concerned about making women visible in the history of education. Christine Mayer had done her research on vocational education in Germany in a historical and gender-oriented perspective. Lea Henriksson looked upon women's involvement in the creation of the Finnish welfare state. Leena Kuusisto and Maija Vesala discussed female teachers as vocational educators in Finland. Anja Heikkinen looked into gendered occupational ideals in Finnish vocational education. I presented my research on the advent of domestic science and housewife ideology in Norwegian education.

We followed this up in a conference in Zurich years later.[2] This focus on women and vocations has been one of the most fascinating features of the Network for me. One of the slogan's of the women's movement was that "the personal is political" and new questions were being raised about women and their place in society both in an historical and sociological perspective. I had been observing and doing research on the traditional gender role divisions in vocational education and training corresponding to the gender role patterns of the manual labour market, featuring the traditional view of women in the family sphere. The social organization of masculinity and feminity has its particular form in vocational education and training. It stands out as a part of "the natural order" to use an expression from Antonio Gramsci. The VET & Culture Network gave me a possibility for sharing and discussing my research in the field. This pattern has been challenging during the past decades and we have seen

1 See Heikkinen, Anja 1996: Gendered History of Vocational Education. European Comparisons. Hämeenlinna: Tampereen Yliopiston Hämeenlinnan Opettajankoulutuslaitos

2 See Gonon, Philipp et al. (eds) 2001: Gender Perspectives on Vocational Education. History, Cultural and Policy Aspects. Bern: Peter Lang

changes, but the main pattern seems to remain, the boys in the "hard fields" and the girls in the caring sector.[3]

However, this problematic is not what I want to highlight here. Here I want to draw attention to that more recently women have presented scientific theories critical of the prevalent ways of thinking in the social sciences during the last century. One general question is whether those scientific perceptions have remained encapsulated within the intellectual traditions that emerged in Western Europe in the sixteenth century, and which saw increased dominance in western capitalistic societies, in spite of the many and constant challenges that the scientific tradition has faced in the 20th century.[4]

In her 1986 book, *The Science Question in Feminism,* Sandra Harding considered these issues from both general and feminist perspectives. As she pointed out, feminists have recently demanded a reshaping of both science and the cultures that legitimize existing science. The book takes as its point of departure the feminist critique that has emerged in opposition to traditional ways of thinking in western scientific theory during the past *decades*. A second point of departure is that the very social structure of science, as well as much of its areas of implementation and technologies, together with the way in which it defines research problems and creates research design, are not only culturally determined, but are also discriminatory in terms of race, class and gender. These problematics have been underlying concerns in the VET & Culture Network since the beginning of our discussions. How to do research where vocational students' and apprentices' voices are heard? How to take people's experience in their everyday life as a point of departure in our research?

I was lucky to spend 2½ years of my life as a visiting scholar at the Ontario Institute for Studies in Education (OISE) in the Department of Sociology of Education in Toronto in the 1980's with feminist scholars Margaret Eichler, Mary O'Brien and Dorothy E. Smith. They had very different points of departures and outlooks in their scientific work. But as Dorothy Smith points out that despite

3 I have presented my research on gender in much of my work. My empirical work on women in the printing industry and change see: Mjelde, in Gonon et al. 2001

4 There is a huge literature that has emerged in this field during the past decades. I just present two thinkers to illustrate my point here; see Mjelde, Liv 1991: Science and Gender. Recent Contributions in Feminist Critical Theory to an Understanding of our Complex Reality. Oslo: Institute of Sociology. University of Oslo.
Beneath Sandra Harding see Smith, Dorothy E. 1987: The Everyday World as Problematic: A Feminist Sociology Toronto: University of Toronto Press. And both Sandra Harding and Dorothy E. Smith has an extensive production in this field during the past decades, but these two books are very important for grasping their basic critique that has inspired me in my work with VET and research.

there will always be many different feminist versions of "reality", what women nevertheless have in common is the organization of social relations that has led to the exclusion of women from the social relations of ruling.

Dorothy Smith has been concerned about ways of doing research that takes people's experience in their everyday lives as a point of departure and with a basic understanding of a political economy from the point of view of the working class. Starting by adopting a women's standpoint, she localizes the thinking reflecting subject as an integral part of the material and historical world being taken as the object of study. And this point of departure also provides an understanding of society's division of labour, of the division between mind and hand as it has developed in the process of industrialization and the distance between on the one hand those who interpret and administrate society and produce the ideas, and on the other, those who apply ideas and produce the material values.

By localizing social scientific work in this way of thinking, we placed ourselves in the standpoint of the working class, from the point where Marx's political economy begins – ourselves entering the scene we are about to analyse. Dorothy Smith states that by no means follows from starting from a women's standpoint that we must begin with people's material reality; but once we have taken these other and decisive steps in our understanding we can begin to examine the relational ways of thinking established by Marx. Social relations then become accessible to us for analysis in the way they were originally conceived, which is to say by locating their premises not in the conceptually abstract world, but in the lives of real individuals, in their work, in their actual, productive activities and the material conditions produced by these activities.

What Smith does is to suggest a method that places those who are the social subjects, not in the role of objects of study, but rather as living thinking individuals, anchored in the everyday world. The title *The Everyday World as Problematic* presents a basis for a sociology that does not begin in discourse, but in real, daily social events between individuals. Smith begins her discussion close to home: how do women organize their domestic and job-related work on a daily and nightly basis? In later years, Smith has broadened her feminist sociology to "a sociology of/for the people". "The Problematic" in the title of her first book encompasses the need to investigate real socially organized relations between experiences in the everyday world and the social relations of capitalism. By using "The Everyday World as Problematic" as a way of thinking, Smith leads us to look for the inner monologue in every person in relation to common traits, order and disorder, opportunities and conditions that are dependent on the person's material reality. Educated populations around the world tend to internalize "capital logic", the ways and outlooks of the ruling apparatus in our shrinking world. Awareness of the hegemonic effect of the relations of ruling, and a shift of emphasis in research toward analyzing our everyday realities is a healthy initiative. Indeed, it places us on the road to building an actual sociology of the people.

New critical contributions by women seem to provide a foundation for ways to understand our complex reality. Their work points toward possibilities for surmounting the traditional division between subject and object, between researcher and researched, between those who interpret society and produce the ideas and those who produce the material values. Dorothy Smith says that social scientists should explain to the members of society how the social organisation works, and in particular those aspects which are not immediately and directly known.[5] These concerns have been underlying our discussions in the VET & Culture Network during the 19 years since our humble beginning in 1993.

## Work, vocationalism and VET – Challenges for a globalised world (Manfred Wahle)

The process of globalisation forces a central challenge for the education system in its whole and with it also to the section of vocational education and training. The tendency of a worldwide division of labour in the production and service sectors as well as in the financial system has directly effects on the structures, organisational principles and processes of the production of goods and services on each national level.

This development has also influence on labour with regard to its institutional structure, organisation, tasks, and content. This is accompanied by a deep change in the demands on human labour in professional live. A high level of flexibility is one central aspect in this context. This is manifested also in watering down the traditional concept of profession and *Beruflichkeit* (vocationalism) – a concept in German speaking area, which is determinant for the vocational education system. Over and above that it has a high importance in different areas like for example social status, career or wages. The different national shaping of the concept of profession has to be taken into account in VET research, as well as the difference in the social perspectives, determined by the historical evolution in each national context.

Although at the moment the process of globalisation cannot be called an unbiased process, it is very significant for labour, profession and education and

5 Smith, Dorothy E. 1974: Women's perspective as a radical critique of Sociology. Sociological Inquiry 44, No.1, 7-13; Smith, Dorothy E. 2005: Institutional Ethnography. A Sociology for People: Lanham: Altamira Press.

with it for vocational education. In this respect the shape of education policy is important for the realization of equal opportunities, transparency, flexibility, variety of opportunity under the condition of globalisation.

Actually, in the context of labour and its basic conditions the question about the concept of profession is very important. For a long time vocationalism was a category to structure the working world as well as vocational learning. In face of the tendency of losing the importance of professional organised labour there is a question about the future of profession and vocationalism and the significant tendency of change. When the future development of the working world in the context of globalisation can be seen under the aspect of vocationalism, the problem comes up, if in a future working world a bundle of functions (still) exist, which acknowledge human activities that refer to a consciousness of vocationalism. Therefore one has to take into account that the profession orders the social status, the income, and the option of further education or career. Thus, the discourse about the future of *Beruf,* profession and vocationalism has far-ranging consequences for vocational-pedagogical research. Its perspective as well as its methodical orientation point to a particular social-scientific access and also to empirical-analytical and social-scientific contextualization.

In this context it is necessary to identify and analyse structural developments which will change the significance and function of VET, and which are exemplary indicators of social megatrends on the one hand and changing processes in the world of work on the other hand. Whereas the effects of globalisation are hardly to forecast in the long run, nevertheless there is evidence that both the significance and function of VET and professional work will change. In this concern there will develop new conditions of VET, and the current principle of vocationalism will erode more or less. According to this scenario, the traditional concept of profession and *Beruflichkeit* (vocationalism) hinders the development of flexible concepts to organize the production and working process.

Because of ongoing globalisation, a central challenge in the sector of VET is to develop models of VET which meet future demands. In this respect it is necessary to stick to the specific national concepts of *Beruflichkeit* which have been developed in different historical and economic structural contexts of a nation. Thus, different national approaches and strategies to cope with new demands of VET in the context of globalisation have to be identified and analysed. The purpose is to discuss the credo, value and sustainability of theoretical and practical solutions. Closely related with this is the perspective to characterise specific processes of inclusion and exclusion in the VET system. This aspect points to questions of class, social discrimination, job discrimination and migration.

Whereas VET systems in European countries and abroad are more or less different, in principle the following aspects are relevant both in national and international contexts:

- the demographic change
- the basic conditions of economy
- the development of the technical production of goods
- the increase of services
- the globalisation of production and financial markets
- the national situation in the process of globalisation.

These aspects are increasingly meaningful for the change of the relationship between vocationalism respectively *Beruflichkeit* and VET. As always the complex relationship between the individual and the world of work is affected, there is way for analytical problems, aiming at the respective problems of particular disciplines: These are, among others, the disciplines of history, sociology, in particular work and occupational sociology or industrial and organizational sociology, as well as (governmental) job market and occupational research. There are also further academic disciplines as well as areas of research and practical work, in which the complicated matter of "humans, work and occupation" is likewise very important. These are, for example, occupational and work laws, occupational medicine and psychology, job counselling or the politics of the job market. In terms of semantic and/or concept-historical questions within this subject the disciplines of philosophy and literary history are concerned.

Therefore, there are countless research fields which are examined in respect of special research interests of different disciplines. However, regarding the content there are intersections between the different research and praxis areas, which means that there is no strict line in definition between them. Even more, each discipline benefits of the proceeds of the others, so in no way they lose their respective independence, but rather keep it. These concerns have been underlying the discussions in the VET & Culture Network since the humble beginnings in 1993.

*The VET & Culture Network (Oslo 2006)*

*Just a process (Hattingen 2010)*

# Coda – Just a Process: Collaborative teaching, research and networking

Collaborative teaching and research is a great concept. It is fostered also by EU policy. The writers of this Festschrift tried to live this idea in our intellectual exchange without funding and any congress machines. Since the beginning of the VET & Culture Network in 1993, one achievement has been the discourse between different local traditions, disciplines and sites of researchers who are involved in Vocational Education and Training.

Nowadays it is quite fashionable to talk about „networks". Indeed, the VET & Culture Network has currently celebrated its 20 years anniversary. This is not spectacular at a first glance. However, the concept and practice of the network is strongly linked to human beings who are willing to work together with others and who see in the encounter with different disciplines, opinions, but also feelings, a worthwhile and valuable activity. So an inter-woven discourse pattern evolved which is more than an internal mutual agreement of the networkers: it also has developed an impact for discussions in Europe. Thus, it is a resource for others outside network. Furthermore young students and researchers are encouraged to follow the course of their intellectual travel and career, and to continue in crossing national borders and thinking modes.

One person has been central for many people who continue to work like this. It is Anja Heikkinen from the North who developed such an enterprise and urged others to engage in these kinds of non-formal and informal debating and writing.

The original idea was to build up a critical mass in order to plan common research projects. But soon we discovered that the debate in an open space with aims for its own sake was even more demanding and satisfying. The aim was not to please potential donors or find external money regardless of the topic, but to define an own research agenda, and an intellectual deliberation. This aim, however, often turns out very demanding and disappointing. Some people stop halfway or behave like free-riders. This is also part of our network-experience.

Anja is an explorer and a person who helped us to find each other, so we achieved a lot. For this we are very grateful to her. She has always kept an independent voice, very suspicious against the official policy talk and the 'Eurobusnocracy', against neo-liberal projects of marketising universities and the commodofication of everything, often disguised by nice words, so typically for 'wordy' politics. But she is also challenging superficial enthusiasm and also popular talks of researchers complaining about the difficulties we meet every day. We have to look beyond myths and brands, as the last conference was titled.

On behalf of the network and all the contributors to this volume we have to express our thanks to Anja for her big and fruitful engagement.

Philipp, Lorenz & Manfred